MasterChef

THE FINALISTS

SERIES 9

MasterChef

THE FINALISTS

DALE WILLIAMS   NATALIE COLEMAN   LARKIN CEN

SERIES 9

A.

Absolute
Press

First published in Great Britain
in 2013 by Absolute Press,
an imprint of Bloomsbury Publishing Plc

Absolute Press
Scarborough House
29 James Street West
Bath BA1 2BT
Phone 44 (0) 1225 316013
Fax 44 (0) 1225 445836
E-mail office@absolutepress.co.uk
Website www.absolutepress.co.uk

Copyright
© Shine TV Limited, 2013
This edition copyright
© Absolute Press, 2013
Foreword copyright
© Thomasina Miers
Photography copyright
© David Loftus, except Thomasina Miers
portrait (page 6), © Karolina Webb

Publisher
Jon Croft
Commissioning Editor
Meg Avent
Art Direction and Design
Matt Inwood
Project Editor
Alice Gibbs
Editor
Norma MacMillan
Photographer
David Loftus
Props Styling
Jo Harris
Food Stylist
Genevieve Taylor
Assistant Food Stylist
Laura Field
Indexer
Ruth Ellis
Proofreader
Zoe Ross

ISBN: 9781906650841

Printed in China by South China Printing
Company.

A note about the text
This book was set using Bembo and Helvetica
Neue. Based on the original designs of
Francesco Griffo, who cut the type used in
1495 by Aldus Manutius to print Cardinal
Bembo's tract, 'De Aetna'. It was updated in
1929 by the Monotype Foundry. Helvetica was
designed in 1957 by Max Miedinger of the
Swiss-based Haas foundry. In the early 1980s,
Linotype redrew the entire Helvetica family.
Helvetica Neue was the result. The typefaces
Clerkenwell and Riverside were used for the
headlines and captions throughout the book.

Bloomsbury Publishing Plc
50 Bedford Square, London WC1B 3DP
www.bloomsbury.com

Shine would like to thank:
Frances Adams, David Ambler, Martin Buckett,
Bev Comboy, John Gilbert, Jessica Hannan,
Lori Heiss, Ben Liebmann, Lisa O'Connell,
Lou Plank, Lyndsey Posner, Franc Roddam,
Karen Ross.

CONTENTS

FOREWORD BY THOMASINA MIERS

If I had been told nine years ago that I would become part of the global phenomenon that is now MasterChef I would not have believed it. I watched the old-style MasterChef when it was presented by Loyd Grossman but when I entered a new format for the show in 2004 I had no idea what to expect. In fact, it is fair to say I had no expectations whatsoever. I had been living in Mexico, was completely broke and had been trying to work out how I could forge a career in food. I completed the entry form on a whim, not without a slight sense of premonition. I didn't tell anyone I had applied, only confessing to my family when suddenly I had to go to an audition just off Great Portland Street in London on one balmy, hot Friday in July.

Competing in that show changed my life. The things we did seem almost old-fashioned now: learning how to ballotine a chicken leg and to decorate petits fours seems pale compared to the molecular wizardry employed by the contestants these days. But the show was new, and the competition was a madly intense experience. Under the careful guidance of Gregg and John we blossomed. They willed us to improve, they bullied us to be better, they never let up for a minute but somehow we knew that this mattered to them, that we weren't just TV fodder. After MasterChef, I went to work in a professional kitchen, something I hadn't envisaged doing before. I don't think I ever would have, had it not been for the encouragement and enthusiasm of Gregg and John.

Nine years later and MasterChef is a global brand, not because it is following a trend that has seen food become increasingly popular every year since its inception, but because the programme is a riveting trial of ordinary people cooking extraordinary things under incredible pressure. When I watch MasterChef contestants soar with incredible feats of cooking prowess, or sink to the occasional lows of the catastrophe, I am gripped by the same emotions that the contestants feel. The tension is palpable, gripping, sometimes unbearable. We sit there willing our favourites to win and marveling at how they withstand horrendous situations and come out triumphant with the most beautiful plates of food.

This year, as ever, the competition appeared fiercer, the cooking more refined; it was an emotional rollercoaster.

It seems unbelievable that a bunch of amateurs could be put through the wringer for a few weeks and then emerge to create such breathtaking works of art that leave even the judges gasping for words.

I adored watching Natalie come through this year, cool as a cucumber and rarely ruffled, consistently producing plates of food ever better than the last. When I was judging the quarter-finals and I tried her Seabass, Fennel and Crab Bonbons I knew I was tasting something that stood out from the crowd, but she continued to surpass herself and I watched with envy as John and Gregg judged her food, wishing that I too were sampling those inspired flavour combinations. She is down to earth but funny, with a natural charm that completely won me over, not to mention the many other millions of viewers who were following her on her journey.

And the competition! Larkin, with his extraordinary feats of cooking, the 'mad professor' of the three, who never held back from pushing the boundaries, always trying to outdo himself with yet another culinary feat. He may not always have pulled it off perfectly but he was going to bust a gut trying and he created some mouth-watering looking dishes. Then there was the technically pitch-perfect Dale with his soft, lilting accent and his consistently beautiful plates of food. His attention to detail was enviable and his food always looked delicious.

We witnessed three very personal journeys of self-improvement with three people who wanted nothing more than to cook to the very best of their ability.

And so it's a real pleasure to be able to follow them on that journey once more through this book, which features all of their recipes from the competition. It also features new recipes from each of them: a mix of innovative and inspiring dishes, and of food intended to comfort and impress in equal measure. It's about the pleasure that food brings and the incredible talents of everyday people. And that, quite simply, is the immensely addictive appeal of MasterChef.

Thomasina Miers
London, July 2013

ABOUT THE RECIPES

The recipes in this book represent the very best of cooking from Series 9 of *MasterChef*. Here, you'll find all of the highlight dishes you'll recognise from the show from the winner, Natalie, and from her fellow finalists, Larkin and Dale. The series goes from strength to strength and the creations of the contestants become more and more wonderful year on year, and these recipes bear testament.

You'll also find an equal quota of new recipes from each of the finalists to enjoy, exclusive to this cookbook. These will be new discoveries and will show you something of the new paths Natalie, Dale and Larkin are embarking on, following the exciting journey of the TV competition which set them on their way.

The TV recipes are clearly flagged throughout the book, for you to quickly reacquaint with old favourites from the series, including each of their three-course final creations, of course.

They are all to be cooked and enjoyed, so go forth and do just that....

Natalie

I hope you enjoy cooking some of the dishes I created for MasterChef and those new ones I created after the competition, especially for this book. Each recipe means a lot to me and has its own special thought process; all are very different from the next.

The two standout dishes from my collection are Pan-Roasted Pigeon with Orange Braised Lentils, Chicory and Hazelnuts (page 52) and Roast Pork Belly, Sous-vide Pork Tenderloin, Black Pudding Scotch Egg (page 44). The Pigeon dish took me over a week to perfect. I spent three or four days planning with my trusty *Flavour Thesaurus* at my side, then practising in the kitchen and correcting. It was the dish that won me a Semi-Final place and made John Torode cry (me too!). It is a very emotional dish.

My pimped up Pork Roast was my winning main course. In hindsight it's a bit of a cheeky dish. But at the time I wanted to show what I love about food and what I love eating; I wanted to refine it into something worthy of a MasterChef Final. I think roast dinner is the best meal of the week and brings back so many happy childhood memories. I also love Scotch eggs. So the two things together is a thoroughly British winning combination!

My grandad's favourite recipe in the book is the Pan-fried Sea Bass with Fennel, Mini Crab Bonbons (page 16). He thinks this dish is world class (his words). He is a massive seafood fan and was my main guinea pig throughout the competition. He gave me lots of constructive criticism (and so many compliments!) during those weeks. He loves his seafood and so his high praise especially for this dish counted every bit as much as the feedback I got from the judges and the previous winners. Grandad is one fussy customer!

PAN-FRIED COD WITH CLAMS,
CHARGRILLED AND PURÉED CAULIFLOWER SERVES 4

This recipe was inspired by my Masterclass with Adam Byatt at Trinity. I had to recreate his signature dish in the Semi-Finals and WOW! what a dish it was. The charred flavour is delicious with the salty samphire, and the lemon purée gives the acidity/sharpness that is needed to balance the rich flavours of the purée. You could also try this recipe with other white fish such as sea bass, or a more meaty fish like halibut.

4 pieces of cod fillet (skin on), about 200g each
rapeseed oil, for frying
a knob of butter
1 sprig of thyme
a squeeze of lemon juice
red vein sorrel, to garnish

For the lemon purée
3 lemons
juice of 1/2 lemon
1 teaspoon caster sugar
2 teaspoons groundnut oil

For the chargrilled cauliflower and cauliflower purée
1 large cauliflower
olive oil
300ml double cream
100ml milk
a small squeeze of lemon juice

For the clams and samphire
24 fresh palourde clams
50g samphire
rapeseed oil
a squeeze of lemon juice
salt and pepper to taste

For the lemon purée. Thinly shave the coloured peel from the lemons, without the white pith. Blanch the peel in a pan of boiling water for 1 minute, then shock in ice-cold water. Repeat the blanching process three times. Put the peel in a spice grinder or mini food processor with the lemon juice, sugar and a pinch of salt. Blitz to a purée, slowly adding the groundnut oil. Set aside.

For the cod. Sprinkle the cod fillets all over with a good pinch of salt, then wrap in clingfilm. Place in the fridge to 'cure' for 30 minutes – the salt will draw out some of the moisture. (While the cod is in the fridge prepare the cauliflower florets for chargrilling and make the cauliflower purée.) Once salted, rinse the cod and dry with kitchen paper.

For the chargrilled cauliflower. Take 12 small florets from the cauliflower and blanch in a pan of boiling water for 3-4 minutes. Drain, then tip into a bowl. Toss with some olive oil and salt. Set aside until needed.

For the cauliflower purée. Finely slice the rest of the cauliflower. Put into a saucepan and cover with the cream and milk. Season well with salt. Bring to the boil, then simmer for 10-15 minutes or until the cauliflower is tender.

Using a slotted spoon transfer the cauliflower to a food processor and blitz until smooth. You might need to add some of the cooking liquid if the purée is too thick. Season well with pepper and add the lemon juice. Set aside in a pan, ready to reheat for serving.

For the clams and samphire. Put the clams and samphire into a saucepan, cover with a lid and steam for 2-3 minutes or until the clam shells have opened. Remove half of the clams from their shells and put them in a bowl with the clams still in shell. Remove the samphire to another bowl and toss with a little rapeseed oil and the lemon juice. Keep warm.

To finish the cod and chargrilled cauliflower. Heat a large frying pan and add some rapeseed oil. Season the cod with pepper, then place skin side down in the pan. Cook for 4 minutes. Turn the cod over, add the butter and thyme sprig to the pan and cook for a further 2-3 minutes, basting the cod with the melted foaming butter. Just as the fish finishes cooking, sprinkle with the lemon juice. Remove from the heat and leave the fish to rest for 1-2 minutes before serving.

Meanwhile, heat a ridged griddle pan and chargrill the cauliflower florets for 1-2 minutes on each side so they are charred.

To serve. Put a big spoonful of cauliflower purée on the top left side of each plate. Set the cod slightly off-centre right, with the clams and chargrilled cauliflower around. Put three blobs of lemon purée at the bottom left of the plate. Scatter the samphire over the cod and clams, garnish with red vein sorrel and finish with a drizzle of rapeseed oil.

Cauliflower and seafood work so well together.

PAN-FRIED SEA BASS WITH CAULIFLOWER PURÉE, CAULIFLOWER COUSCOUS AND TEMPURA CAULIFLOWER   SERVES 4

One of my Semi-Final dishes, inspired by an amazing recipe I once saw. I put a Moroccan twist on the dish, using ras el hanout to delicately season the tempura, and mixing apricots, nuts and fresh herbs into the raw cauliflower couscous. I think the different textures in the dish combine so well – the crunch from the tempura, the freshness of the raw couscous and the smooth, rich purée. People told me that this dish took cauliflower to new heights. It's certainly an underrated vegetable that can be used in so many different ways.

---

4 medium sea bass fillets (skin on),
    about 175g each
olive oil
micro coriander, to garnish

For the cauliflower couscous
1 cauliflower
a handful of almonds (skin on)
a bunch of coriander, finely chopped
a bunch of mint, finely chopped
6 apricots, pitted and finely diced
grated zest and juice of 1/2–1 orange,
    to taste

For the cauliflower purée
florets from 1 large cauliflower
300ml double cream
about 300ml milk
a squeeze of lemon juice

For the tempura cauliflower
oil for deep-frying
50g plain flour
3/4 teaspoon ras el hanout
1 egg, separated
90ml ice-cold water
salt and pepper to taste

For the cauliflower couscous. Preheat the oven to 180°C/Gas Mark 4. Cut the cauliflower vertically in half; reserve one half for the cauliflower tempura. Cut the florets from the remaining cauliflower and put them in a food processor. Blitz to make a couscous-like crumb. Pour into a mixing bowl.

Spread the almonds on a baking tray and roast for 4-5 minutes or until lightly browned. Tip into the food processor and blitz to the same-size coarse crumbs as the cauliflower. Add to the cauliflower in the bowl.

Add the coriander, mint and apricots, followed by orange zest and juice to taste. Mix well and season with salt and pepper. Cover with clingfilm, then leave in the fridge for at least 45 minutes so the flavours infuse.

For the cauliflower purée. Roughly chop the cauliflower florets and put into a saucepan. Pour in the cream and enough milk to cover and add a pinch of salt. Bring to the boil, then simmer for 15-20 minutes or until tender; stir every 5 minutes so the cream doesn't catch on the bottom of the pan. Using a slotted spoon, transfer the cauliflower to a food processor. Add the lemon juice and some pepper, then blitz for 4-5 minutes or until very smooth. You may need to add some of the cooking liquid to loosen the purée, although cauliflower does absorb a lot of liquid during cooking. Set aside in a pan, ready to reheat for serving.

For the tempura cauliflower. Cut 12 small, even-sized florets from the reserved cauliflower half and trim them to neaten. Blanch in a pan of boiling water for 2 minutes. Drain and immerse in iced water for 5 minutes. Remove from the water and drain on kitchen paper.

Heat oil for deep-frying to 180°C. For the batter, combine the flour, ras el hanout, a pinch of salt and a few grinds of pepper in a mixing bowl. Whisk in the egg yolk and ice-cold water to make a smooth batter. In another bowl, whisk the egg white until stiff, then fold into the batter.

Dip the blanched cauliflower florets in the batter, then deep-fry for 2-3 minutes or until golden all over. Drain on kitchen paper to remove excess oil and keep hot.

For the sea bass. Score several small slits, evenly spaced, in the skin of each fillet and trim the ends neatly. Heat a frying pan over medium heat with a little olive oil. Season the skin side of the fish with salt only, then place the fillets skin side down in the pan and cook for 4-5 minutes or until golden and crisp. Season the flesh side with salt and pepper while the fish are cooking. Flip the fillets over and cook for 30-60 seconds, then remove from the heat – the fish will carry on cooking in the residual heat of the pan; you do not want to overcook. Use a fish slice to transfer the fish to kitchen paper to absorb excess oil.

To serve. Make a well of cauliflower purée in the centre of each plate and spoon couscous into the middle. Set the fish on top and garnish with the tempura, micro coriander and a little drizzle of olive oil.

PAN-FRIED SEA BASS WITH FENNEL, MINI CRAB BONBONS AND A SAUCE VIERGE SERVES 4

4 sea bass fillets (skin on), about 175g each
olive oil, for frying
rock salt

For the fennel purée
3 bulbs of fennel, cut lengthways into small
    wedges (fronds reserved for garnish)
1 teaspoon fennel seeds
grated zest of 1 lemon
olive oil
a squeeze of lemon juice

For the fennel confit
1 bulb of fennel, cut lengthways into thin
    slices (fronds reserved for garnish)
1 garlic clove, crushed
3 thin strips of lemon peel (white pith
    removed)
a pinch of Maldon salt
olive oil

For the sauce vierge
1 shallot, finely chopped
2 tablespoons chopped basil
2 plum tomatoes, skinned, deseeded and
    finely diced
a squeeze of lemon juice

For the crab bonbons
125g white crab meat
75g brown crab meat
1/2 red chilli, deseeded and finely chopped
1 tablespoon finely chopped coriander
vegetable oil, for deep-frying
50g plain flour
1 egg, beaten
50g panko breadcrumbs
salt and pepper to taste

For the fennel purée. Preheat the oven to 190°C/Gas Mark 5. Make a foil parcel and add the fennel wedges. Sprinkle with the fennel seeds and lemon zest, season with salt and drizzle over a good glug of olive oil. Seal up the parcel and set it on a baking tray. Bake for 35-40 minutes or until the fennel is soft (check after 25 minutes to make sure the fennel is not getting overcooked).

Transfer all the contents of the fennel parcel to a food processor and blitz to a purée, adding the lemon juice plus a tiny bit more olive oil if needed to loosen the purée. Check the seasoning and adjust if needed. Transfer to a pan, ready to reheat for serving.

For the fennel confit. Place the sliced fennel in a deep pan along with the garlic, lemon peel and Maldon salt. Cover with olive oil and cook over a very low heat for 25-30 minutes or until the fennel is tender – you want to cook it gently so it does not fry. Remove from the oil using a slotted spoon (reserve the oil for the sauce vierge) and drain on kitchen paper. Cover the fennel with foil to keep warm; you want to serve it at room temperature. Set aside.

For the sauce vierge. Put all the ingredients in a saucepan with 100ml oil from the fennel confit and set over a gentle heat to warm for 1-2 minutes. Remove from the heat and set aside to infuse. The sauce can be served warm or at room temperature.

For the crab bonbons. Mix together the white and brown crab meat, chilli and coriander and season with salt and pepper. Roll into eight little balls, just smaller than a 2p coin. Chill in the fridge for about 25 minutes.

Heat oil for deep-frying to 180°C. Set out three bowls on the work surface. Put the flour in one bowl, the egg in the next one and the breadcrumbs in the third. Roll the crab balls in the flour, then dip in the egg and, finally, coat with the breadcrumbs. Deep-fry in the hot oil for 2-3 minutes or until golden brown all over – keep a close eye on them as you only want the breadcrumbs to be golden. Drain on kitchen paper and keep hot (or warm up in a low oven for a few minutes before serving).

For the sea bass. Score the skin of the sea bass and season the skin with salt only. Heat a frying pan until hot, then add a little olive oil and place the fillets in the pan, skin side down. Fry for 4-5 minutes or until the skin is crisp. If the fish starts to shrivel up, remove the pan from the heat for 30 seconds and use a palette knife to hold down and flatten the fish, then return to the heat. Season the flesh side with salt and pepper while the fillets are cooking. When the flesh is nearly all white throughout, flip the fish over and cook for 30-60 seconds, then remove from the heat (the fish will carry on cooking in the residual heat of the pan; you don't want to overcook). Use a fish slice to transfer the sea bass to kitchen paper to remove excess oil. Keep hot.

To serve. Make a teardrop of fennel purée near the top of each plate. Lay a fish fillet on the purée. Add a small line of purée next to this and arrange alternating confit wedges and crab bonbons. Spoon the sauce vierge around the plate and sprinkle a little rock salt on the fish fillet. Garnish with fennel fronds.

I only started eating fennel a few years ago – my mum never cooked with it at home, but since I cooked this dish for her she now loves it as much as I do! All the flavours are fresh and work really well together, and the confit, shaved and puréed fennel all add different textures. Sauce vierge is a classic that complements it all perfectly. I cooked this in the Quarter-Finals, for previous *MasterChef* winners Mat Follas, Thomasina Miers and Peter Bayless, and they really enjoyed it.

SEA BASS CEVICHE WITH POMELO

SERVES 4

I like cooking for my friends and often have them over for dinner. I generally pick a theme and create a menu based around it. I decided on a Mexican theme one night and made a ceviche for the starter, which needed some citrus. Coming home from a night out in Bethnal Green I happened to stop in one of the local shops and saw this huge yellow melon-like thing in a netted bag. I asked the man what it was, and he said it was a pomelo. Out of interest I bought it. The next morning I searched online and found out that the pomelo is a citrus fruit, similar to a grapefruit. I find the flavour a bit sweeter than grapefruit, and it was perfect for my Mexican ceviche.

4 large sea bass fillets, skinned and
   pin-boned
2 pomelos
juice of 2 limes
1 red chilli, finely chopped
4 spring onions, finely chopped
1 tablespoon finely chopped coriander
coriander and rose sea salt (or any other
   sea salt infused with coriander), to taste
pepper to taste
micro coriander, to garnish

Cut the fish into thin strips and place in a large bowl. Set aside.

Peel one of the pomelos (be sure to remove the white pith, too, as it is bitter). Cut out the segments from the membrane. Juice the other pomelo – use a juicing machine or citrus juicer if you can as the pomelo is quite a tough fruit.

Add the pomelo juice to the sea bass along with the lime juice, chilli, spring onions and coriander. Season to taste with the coriander and rose sea salt and pepper. Leave in the fridge for 5-10 minutes or until the flesh starts to turn white.

To serve. Mix the pomelo segments into the sea bass ceviche. Spoon on to the plates and garnish with micro coriander.

A Mexican-themed dish for my friends.

PAN-FRIED SEA BREAM FILLET WITH LANGOUSTINE, BRAISED FENNEL, CARAMELISED FENNEL AND A LANGOUSTINE SAUCE

SERVES 4

MASTERCHEF | THE FINALISTS COOKBOOK

This is the dish I made for the critics in the Semi-Finals, which was the decider to win a place in the Final. I chose to do a classic bisque, which is very elegant and extravagant because of the langoustines. I wanted to show I could do classical dishes, although I had everyone in stitches by the way I pronounced langoustine – 'lan-quist-ging'!

For the fish stock

1kg white fish bones (ideally the bones from the sea bream)
1 carrot, roughly chopped
1 white onion, roughly chopped
1 celery stick, roughly chopped
6 black peppercorns
1 bay leaf
4 parsley stalks

For the langoustine sauce

12 fresh langoustines
olive oil
2 large knobs of unsalted butter
1 carrot, finely chopped
1 celery stick, finely chopped
1 onion, finely chopped
1 bay leaf
3 tablespoons Pernod
2 large plum tomatoes, deseeded and roughly chopped
1 tablespoon tomato purée
100ml double cream

For the braised fennel

2 bulbs of fennel
a knob of butter
a squeeze of lemon juice

For the caramelised fennel

2 bulbs of baby fennel
a large knob of butter
3 tablespoons caster sugar

For the sea bream

4 sea bream fillets (skin on), scaled and pin-boned, about 100g each
1 tablespoon olive oil
25g unsalted butter
a squeeze of lemon juice
salt and pepper to taste

For the fish stock. Chop the fish bones so they will fit in a large pot. Add the rest of the stock ingredients and cover with water. Bring to the boil, then simmer gently for 25 minutes. Strain into a bowl or jug and set aside until needed. (Any stock not used for the langoustine sauce and braised fennel can be frozen.)

For the langoustine sauce. Remove the heads from the langoustines; reserve the heads. Heat a little olive oil with the butter in a large saucepan and, when foaming, add the langoustine tails. Cook for 3–5 minutes or until just firm. Remove from the pan and set aside. Add the reserved heads to the pan and cook over a high heat until browned.

Meanwhile, using scissors and your fingers, carefully remove the langoustine tails from their shells. Reserve the langoustines. Add the shells to the pan with the heads and reduce the heat to low.

In another saucepan, heat a little olive oil and sweat the carrot, celery and onion with the bay leaf until softened. Add the shells from the other pan and stir to mix. Add the Pernod and reduce a little, stirring, then add the tomatoes and tomato purée. Season with a good grinding of black pepper and a little salt, and add 75ml of the fish stock. If the flavour is too intense, add more fish stock, then slowly stir in the cream – you may not need it all, so add a little bit at a time and taste as you go. Once you are happy with the sauce, remove from the heat and leave to infuse for about 45 minutes. Strain through a fine sieve into a clean pan and set aside, ready to reheat gently for serving.

For the braised fennel. Remove the tops, fronds (reserve the fronds for garnish) and cores from each bulb of fennel. Cut lengthways into fine slices. Heat the butter in a frying pan and add the fennel slices along with enough fish stock to cover, the lemon juice and some salt. Cook gently for 30–40 minutes or until tender; keep checking to be sure the fennel isn't catching on the bottom of the pan. When the fennel is ready, drain and keep hot.

For the caramelised fennel. Slice the baby fennel lengthways in half and then into quarters (or eighths if large). Heat the butter in a pan, add the fennel and sprinkle with the sugar. Cook for 3–5 minutes or until the fennel is just tender but still crunchy and is caramelised. Remove from the heat and keep hot.

For the sea bream. Score the skin of the fillets and season with salt. Heat a pan until hot, then add the olive oil followed by the fish, skin side down. Season the flesh side with salt and pepper. When the fish is nearly cooked (flesh almost all white), add the butter, lemon juice and four of the peeled langoustine tails. (Keep the remaining tails in the fridge for 2–3 days to eat with any leftover fennel, or serve them all with the bream.) Season the langoustines when they hit the pan. Flip the fillets over and cook for a further minute, spooning the butter over the fish to give a nice finish. Remove from the pan and leave to rest for 1 minute.

To serve. Spoon the braised fennel in the middle of each soup plate or bowl. Set a sea bream fillet on top of the braised fennel, with a langoustine on top of the fish. Lean the caramelised fennel against the fish. Spoon the langoustine sauce around and garnish with fennel fronds.

PAN-FRIED WILD HALIBUT FILLET, WILD MUSHROOM CONSOMMÉ, WILD MUSHROOMS, TRUFFLE AND SPINACH SERVES 4

I love to spend Saturday mornings wandering around Borough Market. You see things that you won't find in a supermarket. There's a big greengrocer called Turnips which has a really good selection of wild mushrooms and truffles when in season. I got a bit over-excited when I saw these but wasn't sure what to put them with. I looked to my right and there was a big fishmonger. BINGO! Earthy mushrooms and truffle with fish.

4 pieces of halibut fillet, preferably wild halibut (skin on), about 175g each
olive oil, for frying
unsalted butter, for frying
200g fresh spinach
1 black truffle
truffle oil

For the consommé
10g dried porcini
10g dried morels
1 shallot, sliced
25g unsalted butter
1 tablespoon tomato purée
100g mixed fresh wild mushrooms (chanterelles or girolles, enoki, black trumpet)
1 portobello mushroom, chopped into chunks
500ml chicken stock
4 tablespoons Madeira
3 egg whites

For the wild mushrooms
olive oil, for frying
a knob of butter
2 large king oyster mushrooms, cut in half
160g mixed fresh wild mushrooms (chanterelles or girolles, enoki, black trumpet)
2 tablespoons finely chopped flat-leaf parsley
salt and pepper to taste

For the consommé. Put the dried porcini and morels into a bowl, pour over 250ml boiling water and leave to soak for 20 minutes. Soften the shallot in the butter in a large saucepan. Add the soaked mushrooms with their liquid (leave any sandy sediment at the bottom of the bowl) as well as the tomato purée, fresh mushrooms, stock and Madeira. Season with a good pinch of salt and bring to the boil, then reduce the heat and simmer for 1 hour. Strain through a fine sieve into a clean pan (discard the contents of the sieve) and leave to cool.

Whisk the egg whites in a bowl to soft peaks, then add to the cooled consommé and set over a low heat. As you heat the consommé, the egg whites on the surface will gather up the impurities. Once the consommé is clear, skim this 'raft' of egg white off the top. Pass the consommé through a sieve lined with muslin into a clean pan. The consommé will now be crystal clear. Check the seasoning, then set aside, ready to reheat for serving.

For the wild mushrooms. Heat a frying pan and add a glug of olive oil and the butter. Add the king oyster mushrooms and cook until they start to soften. Add the rest of the mushrooms and the parsley and season with salt and pepper. Sauté for 2–3 minutes or until the mushrooms are all softened and slightly

browned. Tip them on to kitchen paper to drain, then keep hot while you cook the fish.

For the halibut. Season the skin side of the fish with salt. Heat some olive oil in a large frying pan and, when hot, place the fillets, skin side down, in the pan. As you brown the skin, season the flesh side with salt and pepper. When the skin is crisp, flip the fish over and slightly brown the flesh side. Cooking should take about 5 minutes in total – you don't want to overcook the fish. For the last minute of cooking, add a big knob of butter, melt it and baste the fish with the foaming butter. Remove from the heat and allow the fish to rest for a minute before serving.

For the spinach. While the fish is resting, heat a saucepan and add a little olive oil and a big knob of butter. Add the spinach and wilt it. Season with salt, then drain on kitchen paper to absorb the excess liquid.

To serve. Put a pile of spinach in the middle of each soup plate or bowl. Set a halibut fillet on top, skin side down. Arrange the king oysters around the fillet and scatter the mixed mushrooms over and around the fish. Ladle in the hot consommé. To finish, shave a few pieces of truffle over the dish and drizzle with a tiny bit of truffle oil.

Earthy mushrooms and truffle with fish: yum!

SQUID WITH SQUID INK SAUCE, SERRANO HAM CRISPS, FENNEL POLLEN AND FENNEL SERVES 4

This recipe was inspired by a meal I had with Dale and Larkin the night I won *MasterChef*. We celebrated in a tapas restaurant and had cuttlefish with squid ink, something I'd never eaten before. The Serrano ham crisps add a texture contrast to the dish, and complement the squid.

100g Serrano ham (medium sliced)
12 baby squid, cleaned and tentacles
   reserved
olive oil, for frying and dressing
2 teaspoons fennel pollen
juice of 1 lemon

For the squid ink sauce
1 onion
2 garlic cloves
2 celery sticks
1 bulb of fennel
1 tablespoon olive oil
100ml Pedro Ximenez sherry
400ml fish stock
1 tablespoon tomato purée
4g squid ink

For the chargrilled fennel
1 bulb of fennel (with fronds)
grated zest of 1 lemon
1 tablespoon olive oil
salt and pepper to taste

For the squid ink sauce. Roughly chop the onion, garlic, celery and fennel, then soften in the olive oil in a saucepan. Add the sherry and reduce by a third. Add the fish stock, tomato purée and squid ink and season with a good grinding of pepper. Bring to the boil, then reduce the heat and simmer for about 20 minutes.

Pass through a sieve into a clean pan. If the sauce is too thin (you want it to be thick enough to coat the back of a spoon), return to the heat and boil to reduce further. Check the seasoning, adding a little salt if needed. Set aside, ready to reheat for serving.

For the Serrano ham crisps. Preheat the oven to 180°C/Gas Mark 4. Cut the ham into triangles (you want 12) and lay out on a baking tray lined with baking parchment. Cover with another sheet of parchment and set another baking tray on top to weight down the ham. Bake for 7–10 minutes or until crisp. Set aside.

For the chargrilled fennel. Reserve the fennel fronds for garnish. Cut the fennel bulb lengthways into eight equal wedges. Put them in a bowl. Add the lemon zest and olive oil and season with salt and pepper. Turn the wedges to coat well. Heat a ridged griddle pan until very hot, then chargrill the fennel wedges until tender, turning them occasionally. Transfer to a plate and keep warm.

For the squid. Slice each squid body up its back and open out flat. Using the back of the knife, scrape the inside in case there is any dirt or sand. Turn the pieces over and, using a serrated knife, score the squid in a criss-cross pattern. Rinse the squid and tentacles under cold running water, then pat dry with kitchen paper.

Put the squid and tentacles in a mixing bowl and drizzle over a good glug of olive oil. Add the fennel pollen and season with salt. Using your hands, mix well so the fennel pollen coats all the squid.

Heat an unoiled frying pan until very hot, then drop in the squid. It will curl up. After a minute remove from the heat and tip the squid on to a cutting board. Chop the squid into slices, then return to the pan and cook for another minute or so. Add the lemon juice and a grinding of pepper, and dress with a little more olive oil. Remove from the heat.

To serve. Spoon a tablespoon of the squid ink sauce on the left hand side of each plate and arrange the squid on top. Place two fennel wedges on the right hand side. Add three Serrano ham crisps to each plate. Drizzle another tablespoon of squid ink sauce around each plate and garnish with fennel fronds.

CORIANDER AND ORANGE PAN-FRIED SCALLOPS
WITH BEETROOT PURÉE, BEETROOT WEDGES AND SAMPHIRE SERVES 4

John said he had never eaten this ingredient combination before. Scallops are very sweet and I wanted to put them with something earthy, but not a traditional partner. Beetroot, one of my all-time favourite vegetables, was a great idea, with orange to mellow the earthy flavour. When devising a dish I normally start with the star of the show – in this case the scallops – and plan around it, but my starting block here was the beetroot and orange.

For the beetroot purée and wedges
4½ cooked natural beetroots, peeled
juice of 1 orange
½ teaspoon coriander seeds, crushed
olive oil

For the vinaigrette
5 tablespoons olive oil
1 tablespoon red wine vinegar

For the samphire
50g samphire
olive oil

For the scallops
12 diver-caught scallops, cleaned,
  without roes
olive oil, for frying
½ teaspoon coriander seeds, crushed
a good squeeze of orange juice
salt and pepper to taste

To garnish
micro coriander
zest of 1 orange

For the beetroot purée and wedges. Preheat the oven to 180°C/Gas Mark 4. Put the whole beetroots into a bowl with the orange juice and coriander seeds and turn to coat. Leave to marinate for 10 minutes. Make a foil parcel and place the beetroots inside, then drizzle over some olive oil and a little of the marinade (reserve the remainder for the vinaigrette). Season with salt and pepper, then close the parcel and set on a baking tray. Roast for 20-25 minutes.

Reserve one and a half of the beetroots for the wedges. Chop the other three beetroots into rough 3cm chunks and put into a food processor with the juices from the foil parcel. Blitz to a purée, adding a little olive if the purée is too thick. Pass through a sieve into a pan and set aside ready to reheat for serving. Make sure you check the seasoning and adjust if needed.

Cut the reserved beetroots into 12 wedges. Set aside until needed.

For the vinaigrette. Strain the reserved beetroot marinade. In a small bowl, whisk 4 tablespoons of the strained marinade with the olive oil, vinegar and a pinch of salt. Set aside.

For the samphire. Drop the samphire into a pan of boiling water and blanch for 1-2 minutes – you want the samphire still to have bite. Drain and place in a small mixing bowl. Dress the samphire with a little olive oil. Season with a crack of pepper only, as samphire is naturally salty. Set aside.

For the scallops. Put the scallops in a mixing bowl, drizzle on a little olive oil and add the coriander seeds. Mix well. Heat a frying pan and, when hot, place the scallops in the pan and cook for 1-2 minutes on each side. When they are nearly cooked, add a good squeeze of orange juice to deglaze.

To serve. Make a teardrop of beetroot purée on each plate and set the scallops on top. Add the wedges of beetroot, samphire and drizzles of vinaigrette and garnish with micro coriander. Finish by grating the orange zest over the plates.

My starting block here was the beetroot and orange.

Making Coriander and Orange Pan-fried Scallops with Beetroot Purée, Beetroot Wedges and Samphire, (see page 26)

MASTERCHEF | THE FINALISTS COOKBOOK

NATALIE COLEMAN

The orange and hazelnut vinaigrette
really wakes up the whole dish.

SCALLOPS WITH JERUSALEM ARTICHOKES AND HAZELNUTS SERVES 4

This idea came to me after eating at Viajante in Bethnal Green. I had their pig's trotters with artichokes. There were different textures of artichokes: crisps, purée and fermented. The combination was very interesting so I thought about what artichokes go with and decided to pair them with sweet scallops, and added hazelnuts to bring a nutty flavour.

20g blanched (skinned) hazelnuts
rapeseed oil, for frying
12 large scallops (without roe)
a knob of butter
a squeeze of lemon juice
red amaranth, to garnish

For the Jerusalem artichoke purée
250g Jerusalem artichokes, cut into 2cm
   pieces
50ml milk
100ml double cream
a squeeze of lemon juice

For the vinaigrette
1 tablespoon groundnut oil
1 tablespoon hazelnut oil
1 tablespoon orange balsamic vinegar

For the Jerusalem artichoke crisps
vegetable oil, for deep-frying
1 large Jerusalem artichoke
salt and pepper to taste

For the Jerusalem artichoke purée. Put the artichokes in a saucepan with the milk and cream. Season with salt. Simmer for 15-20 minutes or until the artichokes are tender, stirring frequently to make sure the cream doesn't catch on the bottom of the pan. Transfer to a food processor. Add the lemon juice and a few grinds of pepper, then blitz to a smooth purée. Check the seasoning. Set aside in a pan, ready to reheat for serving.

For the hazelnuts. Toast the hazelnuts in a dry frying pan until you start to smell them. Cool, then tip into a food processor or spice blender and blitz until roughly chopped. You want a mixture of chunks and nearly ground. Set aside.

For the vinaigrette. Whisk together the oils and vinegar. Season and set aside.

For the Jerusalem artichoke crisps. Heat oil for deep-frying to 160°C. Finely slice the artichoke on a mandolin (you want 12 nice slices). Fry in the hot oil, in batches, until lightly browned – this will take less than a minute so watch carefully as the crisps can burn very quickly. Remove with a slotted spoon and drain on kitchen paper. Season with salt. Set aside.

For the scallops. Heat a large frying pan and add some rapeseed oil. Season the scallops with salt, then place in a circle in the pan. Cook for 1-2 minutes or until nicely seared on the bottom. Flip them over, in the order you put them in the pan. Add the butter and cook for another 1-2 minutes, basting the scallops with the melted foaming butter. Add the lemon juice, then remove the scallops from the pan and put on to a plate to rest for a minute before serving.

To serve. Put three blobs of purée on each plate. Place a scallop on top of each dollop and set a crisp on each scallop. Scatter the hazelnuts over the plates, then drizzle the vinaigrette around. Garnish with red amaranth.

CRAB-FILLED COURGETTE FLOWERS WITH LEMON MAYONNAISE SERVES 4

On one of my regular Saturday visits to Borough Market I found that courgette flowers were in season and bought a bunch to try. I knew that crab works well with courgettes and decided to add some mint, chilli and ricotta to make a fresh-tasting filling for the flowers. For an alternative dip to mayo, mix a little crème fraîche with grated lemon zest and juice.

For the courgette flowers
150g white crab meat
50g brown crab meat
50g ricotta
grated zest of 1/2 lemon
1 red chilli, finely diced
leaves from 2 sprigs of mint, finely chopped
8 courgette flowers

For the mayonnaise
1 egg yolk
1/2 teaspoon Dijon mustard
1/2 garlic clove, crushed
150ml light, mild olive oil
1 teaspoon white wine vinegar
grated zest and juice of 1/2 lemon

For the batter
100g cornflour
150g self-raising flour
10g baking powder
300–400ml sparkling water
vegetable oil, for deep-frying
salt and pepper to taste

To garnish
Maldon salt
micro coriander

For the courgette flowers. Combine the white and brown crab meat, the ricotta, lemon zest, red chilli and mint in a mixing bowl and mix together. Season well with salt and pepper. Fill each flower with the crab mixture – do not overfill or they will burst when cooking. Chill in the fridge for 30 minutes to set.

For the mayonnaise. Make the mayonnaise while the courgette flowers are in the fridge. Put the egg yolk, mustard, garlic, a good pinch of salt and a few grinds of black pepper into a bowl. Start to whisk, adding the oil a few drops at a time. When the mixture starts to thicken add the vinegar, then continue whisking in the oil. You can do this a bit more quickly, but don't add it too fast or the mixture will split. Once all the oil has been added, whisk in the lemon zest and juice. You may want to adjust the seasoning according to taste, to bring out the lemon flavour.

For the batter. Mix together the cornflour, self-raising flour and baking powder in a bowl. Gently whisk in the sparkling water, adding just enough to make a smooth batter.

Heat oil for deep-frying to 180°C. Fry the courgette flowers in batches so the pan isn't crowded: dip each flower into the batter to coat, then gently add to the hot oil and fry for 3-4 minutes or until the batter is crisp and golden. Remove and drain on kitchen paper.

To serve. Place two courgette flowers on each plate with a dollop or small bowl of lemon mayonnaise. Add a sprinkling of Maldon salt and garnish with micro coriander.

The contrast of soft gooey filling with the crisp tempura coating is very good!

LOBSTER TAIL, FENNEL PURÉE, COMPRESSED FENNEL, ORANGE GEL, ORANGE BEURRE BLANC, LOBSTER CAVIAR AND LOBSTER OIL   SERVES 4

FROM THE SERIES, FINAL DISH

I made this as my starter for the Final. I always knew that if I got to the last stage I would have to use a luxury ingredient like lobster. I decided on a classical approach, with orange and fennel prepared three ways to add different textures and flavour. It seemed a crime to throw out the lobster shells, so I used them to make a lobster oil to add more depth to the dish. After cooking with Simon Rogan and also Chef Luca at Enoteca Pinchiorri, I became interested in molecular cookery. I decided to try using fancy kitchen gadgets and techniques in the Final. Some of the fennel is vacuum-packed forcing in the flavour of mandarin oil, and the subtle gel adds a nice mellow orange element to the dish without overpowering it as orange segments or zest would.

4 live lobsters, about 500g each
Maldon salt
50g unsalted butter
lobster caviar, to garnish

For the lobster oil
250ml mild, light olive oil
2 pieces of orange peel
1 sprig of tarragon

For the orange gel
1 gelatine leaf
200ml fresh orange juice
25g caster sugar
1g agar agar

For the compressed fennel
1 bulb of fennel
50ml mandarin-flavoured oil or orange-flavoured oil (shop-bought)

For the fennel purée
2 bulbs of fennel
about 4 tablespoons olive oil
grated zest of 1/2 orange
a squeeze of orange juice

For the shaved fennel
1/2 bulb of fennel
1 1/2 teaspoons olive oil
a squeeze of orange juice

For the orange beurre blanc
grated zest and juice of 1 orange
50g unsalted butter
leaves picked from 1 sprig of tarragon, finely chopped
salt and pepper to taste

For the lobster. Leave the lobsters in the freezer for 30 minutes to 1 hour. Bring a large pot of water to the boil, adding 1 tablespoon Maldon salt for every litre of water. Push the tip of a large, sharp knife through the head to kill each lobster, then put it, head first, into the boiling water. Cook for 12 minutes. Remove from the pan and plunge into iced water, then drain and leave to cool for 15-20 minutes.

Separate the tails from the bodies. Using sturdy scissors, cut along the shell of each tail on the underside (or you can break the shells apart with your hands if the shells are not too tough). Remove the lobster tail meat in one piece; set aside until ready to finish for serving. Reserve the tail shells and everything else for the lobster oil.

Before serving the lobster tails, heat the butter in a large frying pan along with a glug of the lobster oil, add the tails and gently warm through, basting with the buttery oil. You don't want to cook the lobsters further, just heat them. Lift out

of the pan and set on kitchen paper to remove excess fat.

For the lobster oil. Remove all the guts and the meat from the lobster shells (add the meat to pasta dishes and salads; it can be kept for 3 days in the fridge). Using sturdy scissors, cut the shells into 5cm pieces. Put all the shells into a stockpot with a splash of the olive oil and cook on a gentle heat for 10-15 minutes to colour a bit. Add the rest of the olive oil, the orange peel and tarragon. Cover and simmer over a gentle heat for 1 hour to infuse.

Strain the oil through a conical sieve lined with muslin. Make sure every bit of shell has been removed. Once cool, transfer the oil to a squeezy bottle. This is a strong infusion so you only need a little. The rest will keep in the fridge for a while.

For the orange gel. Soak the gelatine in cold water for about 10 minutes to soften. Combine the orange juice, sugar, agar agar and 50ml water in a saucepan and bring to the boil. Squeeze excess water from the gelatine, then add to the pan and whisk until melted. Pour into a jug. Cool, then chill in the refrigerator to set. Just before serving, loosen the gel with a hand blender.

continued on page 36

continued from page 35

For the compressed fennel. Trim the top and bottom off the fennel bulb (reserve the fronds) and remove the outer layers as they are tough. Cut the fennel bulb lengthways in half, then finely slice the halves lengthways on a mandolin. Put the fennel in a vacuum bag with the mandarin oil, seal and compress three times. Leave to infuse for 45 minutes to get the flavour of the oil into the fennel. If you do not have a vacuum-pack machine you can pack the fennel and oil in a food bag and seal it, or use a sealed plastic box.

For the fennel purée. Trim the top and bottom off the bulb of fennel and remove the outer leaves, which are tough. Cut lengthways into wedges and place in a foil parcel with the olive oil and orange zest and juice. Seal the parcel and set it on a baking tray. Bake for 30-40 minutes or until the fennel is soft. Tip the contents of the foil parcel into a food processor and blitz for 4-5 minutes or until very smooth; you may need to add a little more olive oil to loosen the purée. Season with pepper and salt to taste. Put into a pan, ready to reheat for serving.

For the shaved fennel. Trim the top and bottom off the bulb of fennel and remove the outer leaves, which are tough. Very finely slice lengthways on a mandolin. Dress the fennel slices with the oil and orange juice. Set aside.

For the orange beurre blanc. Put the orange zest and juice in a small pan and bring to the boil. Whisk in the butter, then remove from the heat and add the chopped tarragon. Keep warm.

To serve. Make a teardrop of fennel purée off-centre left on each plate. Next to it, on the right side, arrange the compressed fennel. Place a lobster tail in the centre. Add blobs of orange gel around the plate. Scatter some shaved fennel around the plate. Drizzle orange beurre blanc over the lobster and around the plate. Put $1/2$ teaspoon of lobster caviar on top of each lobster tail. Garnish with the reserved fennel fronds. Finish with a drizzle of lobster oil.

Describe your first food memory...

It would have to be a typical Sunday afternoon with all my family. Sundays were always full of eating. In the morning my dad would take me and my sister to Brick Lane to buy beigels; when we got home my mum would make bacon beigels for breakfast. Then we would all go to my nan's for Sunday roast, which was followed by a huge choice of desserts. And then later we'd have afternoon tea, with her famous corned beef hash pie.

Thoughts on your co-finalists?

They are great guys. Larkin is like a mad professor with all his kitchen gadgets. It wouldn't surprise me if he invents one himself! Dale is the most technical of the three of us, and his food always looks like something from a fine dining restaurant.

A classically English flavour combination in an Italian dish.

BEETROOT AND GOAT'S CHEESE RISOTTO

SERVES 4

I tend to go through major cravings, but beetroot is always one of them! Sometimes I just have to eat beetroot or drink beetroot juice. Sounds very strange, I know... Inspired by the wonderful food we ate on Italy's Amalfi coast, I thought why not blend together a classically English flavour combination of beetroot and goat's cheese with a risotto. So I did, and it worked.

50g unsalted butter
1 tablespoon olive oil
1 leek, white part only, finely sliced
1 white onion, finely diced
2 garlic cloves, crushed
picked leaves from 4 sprigs of thyme
400g fresh beetroots, peeled and cubed
900ml vegetable or chicken stock
300g risotto rice
250ml white wine
juice of 1 lemon
3 tablespoons finely chopped parsley
2 tablespoons crème fraîche
50g pecorino or Parmesan, freshly grated
200g goat's cheese
salt and pepper to taste

To garnish
pea shoots
50g goat's cheese, crumbled
extra virgin olive oil

Melt the butter with the oil in a saucepan and add the leek, onion, garlic, thyme and beetroot. Cook for 4–5 minutes or until the leek and onion have softened (you don't want them to brown).

Meanwhile, heat the stock in a separate pan, without boiling, then keep it on a low heat.

When the vegetables are soft, add the rice and mix well. Cook for a few minutes, then add the wine and lemon juice. Bubble until most of the liquid has been absorbed. Add a ladleful of the hot stock to the rice, stir it in and continue to stir as the rice cooks. When the stock has been absorbed, add another ladleful. Continue adding the hot stock in this way, waiting for each addition to be absorbed before adding the next. You need to keep stirring constantly during the cooking. When all the stock has been added, the rice will be plumped but still a little al dente.

Add the chopped parsley, crème fraîche and pecorino and crumble in the goat's cheese. Fold gently into the risotto. Remove from the heat and season with salt and pepper (taste the risotto before adding salt, as the cheese will bring saltiness to it).

To serve. Spoon the risotto into bowls. Garnish with pea shoots and goat's cheese and add a drizzle of extra virgin olive oil. Finish with a grinding of black pepper.

BUTTERNUT SQUASH AND MASCARPONE PAPPARDELLE SERVES 4

This recipe was inspired by my visit to Mamma Agata's cookery school where we worked with a small number of great ingredients. Butternut squash and pine nuts is a favourite pairing of mine, so I focused on these to make a homely, simple, tasty pasta dish. If you don't feel confident about making your own pappardelle, you can use shop-bought pasta instead, but try to buy the best quality.

For the pasta
400g type 00 flour, plus a little extra for rolling
4 eggs

For the sauce
1 butternut squash, about 700g
2 medium red onions, peeled
1 red chilli, deseeded and finely sliced (optional)
olive oil
1 tablespoon dried rosemary and sage *or* leaves from 1 sprig of rosemary and 4 torn sage leaves
50g pine nuts
250g mascarpone
salt and pepper to taste

To finish
freshly grated Parmesan
extra virgin olive oil

For the pasta. Put the flour on a clean work surface, make a well and crack in the eggs. Using a fork, whisk the eggs together, then slowly incorporate the flour. Once mixed to a dough, knead for about 5 minutes or until firm. Wrap in clingfilm and leave in the fridge to rest for 1 hour.

Cut the piece of dough in half; set one half aside. Using a rolling pin, start to roll out the dough into a rectangle to flatten it a bit. Then roll it through a pasta machine until it is very thin. Flour the sheet of dough every time you put it through the machine, to prevent it from sticking. When rolled thin enough, cut into 2cm strips. Repeat with the remaining dough. Toss the strips with flour to prevent them from sticking together, then set aside.

For the sauce. Preheat the oven to 180°C/Gas Mark 4. Peel the butternut squash and cut into 2cm chunks, discarding the seeds. Place in a baking tray. Cut each red onion into eight wedges and add to the baking tray with the chilli, if using. Drizzle over a good glug of olive oil and scatter on the rosemary and sage. Season with salt and pepper. Bake for 40-45 minutes or until the squash is tender.

Meanwhile, toast the pine nuts in a frying pan for about 1 minute or until they start to turn golden. Tip on to a plate and leave to cool.

To finish and serve. Bring a large pan of salted water to the boil. Add the pasta and cook for 3-5 minutes or until al dente. Drain, reserving a little of the cooking water.

Heat the mascarpone in a large sauté pan. When it starts to melt add the butternut squash mixture. Then add the pine nuts and cooked pasta. If the mixture is a little thick add 2-3 tablespoons of the reserved cooking water. Season with a little salt and a good grinding of pepper. Serve immediately, topped with freshly grated Parmesan and a drizzle of olive oil.

Sometimes just a few great ingredients can make such a tasty dish.

BRAISED PIG'S CHEEKS WITH CELERIAC PURÉE, CRACKLING AND BLACKBERRIES SERVES 4

Out shopping in Columbia Road market, I went into an old-fashioned sweet shop. A jar of twigs by the cashier turned out to be liquorice root. I thought about how I could use this in my cooking and decided it would work well in a sauce. I knew that liquorice and pork worked together, so I paired the liquorice with braised pig's cheeks and added blackberries to cut through the richness of the meat and add a freshness to the dish, along with the garnish of pea shoots.

For the pig's cheeks
8 pig's cheeks
50g seasoned flour
olive oil, for frying
1 leek, white part only, finely sliced
1 large white onion, roughly chopped
2 celery sticks, roughly chopped
2 carrots, roughly chopped
100ml Madeira
400ml red wine
450ml chicken stock
1 star anise
1 liquorice root stick, broken in half
4 sprigs of thyme
a knob of unsalted butter
juice of 1/2 lemon

For the crackling
350g pork skin

For the celeriac purée
1 celeriac (about 400g), peeled and
   chopped into 2cm chunks
250ml whole milk
250ml double cream
salt and pepper to taste

To garnish
12 blackberries, at room temperature
pea shoots

For the pig's cheeks. Preheat the oven to 160°C/Gas Mark 3. Trim any sinew or excess fat from the cheeks. Dust the cheeks with the seasoned flour. Heat a frying pan with some olive oil and brown the cheeks on both sides. Transfer them to a casserole.

Heat a little olive oil in a saucepan and soften the leek, onion, celery and carrots. Add to the cheeks. Pour the Madeira and red wine into the saucepan and boil to reduce by a third. Add to the cheeks along with the chicken stock, star anise, liquorice root and thyme. Season with salt and pepper. Place in the oven and cook for 2 1/2-3 hours or until the cheeks are tender and nearly falling apart. (Prepare the crackling while the cheeks are in the oven.)

Remove the cheeks and place on a plate; keep warm. Pass the cooking liquor through a sieve into a clean saucepan and boil to reduce until thickened. Finish with the butter and lemon juice. Set aside, ready to reheat for serving.

For the crackling. Remove any excess fat from the fleshy side of the skin – you want the crackling to be as crisp as possible. Cut into 1cm strips. Place on a rack over a bowl and pour boiling water from the kettle over them. Dry completely with kitchen paper, then season with salt. Spread out on a baking tray. Place in the oven along with the pig's cheeks and cook for 1-1 1/2 hours until crisp.

For the celeriac purée. Make this while the pig's cheeks and crackling are in the oven. Put the chunks of celeriac in a saucepan with the milk and cream. The celeriac should be submerged in liquid so if necessary add water to top up. Season with a good pinch of salt. Cook for 25-30 minutes or until tender.

Using a slotted spoon, transfer the celeriac to a food processor. Add a few tablespoons of the cooking liquid, then blitz until smooth. You may need to add a little more of the cooking liquid if the purée is too thick. Season with pepper and add more salt if needed. Keep warm.

To serve. Spoon a big blob of celeriac purée on the bottom left hand side of each plate and swipe up with the back of a spoon to make a tear shape. Place two cheeks at the other end of the purée. Dot the blackberries around the pig's cheeks. Drizzle the reduced sauce over the cheeks. Garnish with crackling and pea shoots.

ROAST PORK BELLY, SOUS-VIDE PORK TENDERLOIN, BLACK PUDDING SCOTCH EGG,

POMME PURÉE, CARAMELISED BABY SHALLOTS, SAVOY CABBAGE, APPLE SAUCE AND HONEY MUSTARD SAUCE SERVES 4

Some people have suggested it was a bit cheeky for me to cook a 'pimped-up' Sunday roast for the Final. However, it wasn't intended to be that at all. It was to showcase what we Brits love and are famous for – the Sunday Roast. Scotch egg is another thing that I love, and I added black pudding to the sausagemeat for extra richness. I practised the quail's egg twice at home but didn't master it, so when the egg yolk was runny I was so relieved. Using the sous-vide to cook the pork tenderloin was another risk as it was the first time I had tried it, but I wanted to show I was willing to try new techniques.

1 x 600g piece pork belly
olive oil, for drizzling
leaves picked from 4 sprigs of thyme
pea shoots, to garnish

For the honey mustard sauce
olive oil, for frying
1 pig's trotter, split and chopped into 6 pieces
1kg pork offcuts and bones (ask the butcher for these)
1 sprig of thyme
200g pork mince
500ml chicken stock
1 large white onion, roughly chopped
1 large carrot, roughly chopped
1 bay leaf
2 tablespoons wholegrain mustard
1 tablespoon honey
a knob of unsalted butter

For the apple sauce
2 big Bramley apples, peeled, cored and roughly chopped
juice of 1/2 lemon
50g unsalted butter
1 teaspoon caster sugar

For the black pudding Scotch eggs
4 quail's eggs
3 tablespoons white wine vinegar
150g black pudding, roughly chopped
300g pork sausagemeat
seasoned flour

2 eggs, beaten
fine dry breadcrumbs (natural)
oil for deep-frying

For the caramelised shallots
12 baby shallots, peeled
250ml chicken stock
a knob of unsalted butter

For the sous-vide pork tenderloin
1 large pork tenderloin (fillet), about 600g, trimmed (reserve the trimmings for the sauce)
150ml good-quality apple cider
a knob of unsalted butter

For the pomme purée
800g large Maris Piper potatoes
a handful of Maldon salt
50g unsalted butter
75ml double cream

For the cabbage
100g Savoy cabbage, finely sliced
a knob of butter
salt and pepper to taste

For the honey mustard sauce. Heat a little olive oil in a frying pan and brown the trotter, pork offcuts and bones, and the trimmings from the tenderloin with the sprig of thyme. Tip into a pressure cooker. Brown the pork mince in the same frying pan, adding a bit more olive oil if necessary. You want the mince to be a bit crispy. Deglaze the pan with a little of the chicken stock, then add to the pressure cooker. Soften the onion and carrot in the frying pan with a little more olive oil for 5 minutes. Add to the pressure cooker along with the rest of the chicken stock and the bay leaf. Bring up to pressure and cook on the hob for 1 hour. (If you don't have a pressure cooker, you can use a large stock pot, covered tightly. Cooking time will be 2–3 hours – check the depth of flavour after 2 hours.)

Strain through a sieve into a clean pan; discard the contents of the sieve. Bring to the boil and boil to reduce by half. Add the mustard and honey and finish with the butter and a good grinding of pepper. Set aside, ready to reheat for serving.

For the roast pork belly. Preheat the oven to 160°C/Gas Mark 3. Score the skin of the pork belly using a Stanley knife, or ask your butcher to do this for you. Pat dry, then season the flesh side with salt and pepper. Drizzle olive oil over the skin and sprinkle with salt and the thyme leaves, rubbing these into the skin and pressing into the scores. Place skin side up in a baking tray and roast for 1 1/2 hours.

continued on page 46

continued from page 44

Turn the oven up to 190°C/Gas Mark 5 and roast for a further 25 minutes. If the crackling is not crisp enough, remove it from the belly and roast for 10 more minutes. Leave the pork belly to rest, covered with foil, for 15 minutes before carving. (While the belly is roasting, prepare the remaining elements of the dish.)

For the apple sauce. Put the apples into a saucepan with 5 tablespoons water and the lemon juice. Cook gently for 10-15 minutes or until the apples collapse. Whisk in the butter and sugar, and season with salt and pepper. Set aside, ready to reheat for serving (or you can serve the sauce cold if you prefer).

For the black pudding Scotch eggs. Bring a saucepan of water to the boil. Add 1 tablespoon salt and the quail's eggs and cook for 1 minute 55 seconds. Remove the eggs and plunge them into a bowl of iced water. Add the vinegar to the bowl and set aside in the fridge for 1 hour (to make the eggs easier to peel).

Put the black pudding and sausagemeat in a food processor and blitz until well mixed together. Shape the mixture into four small balls and flatten out on a sheet of clingfilm. Peel the eggs, then carefully wrap in the black pudding mixture, moulding into four smooth balls. Keep in the fridge until needed.

Before serving, dust with seasoned flour, then dip into beaten egg and, finally, coat with breadcrumbs. Heat oil for deep-frying to 180°C. Fry the Scotch eggs for 3-4 minutes or until golden brown all over. Drain on kitchen paper and keep hot.

For the caramelised shallots. Put the peeled shallots in a saucepan with the chicken stock. Bring to the boil, then simmer for 25-30 minutes or until softened. Drain. Carefully slice the shallots vertically in half and set aside. Before serving, reheat in a pan with the butter to caramelise the cut surface and season to taste.

For the sous-vide tenderloin. Season the tenderloin with salt and pepper, then put into a vacuum bag with the cider and cook in a water bath at 68°C for 1 hour. (If you don't have a vacuum-pack machine and a water bath, you can use a deep saucepan, a digital thermometer and some clingfilm. Marinate the tenderloin in the cider overnight, then tightly wrap in three layers of clingfilm. Pierce the clingfilm with a skewer to release any air before wrapping up in a final thin layer of clingfilm to seal. Heat a deep saucepan of water to 68°C, then reduce the heat to maintain this temperature. Place the parcel into the pan of water and cook for 45 minutes to 1 hour, monitoring the temperature the whole time with the thermometer.)

When the tenderloin is cooked (you want to serve it a little pink), remove it from the vacuum bag or clingfilm. Heat the butter in a frying pan and lightly brown the tenderloin on all sides. Season to taste, then keep hot.

For the pomme purée. Put the whole, unpeeled potatoes into a pan of boiling water, add the Maldon salt and cook for 40-50 minutes or until softened. Drain. When cool enough to handle, peel the potatoes, then press through a potato ricer into a pan or bowl. Heat the butter

with the cream in a pan, then whisk into the potatoes. Season with salt and pepper. Keep hot.

For the cabbage. Blanch the cabbage in a pan of boiling water for 3 minutes, then drain well. Just before serving, heat in a pan with the butter and season with salt and pepper.

To serve. Cut the pork belly into four neat rectangles. Slice the tenderloin on the diagonal and portion into four. Make a teardrop shape of pomme purée on each plate, going into the centre. Set the pork belly in the centre. At 2 o'clock put a Scotch egg; at 5 o'clock arrange the tenderloin slices. Place the shallots randomly in and around the other elements. Put the apple sauce in a small serving pot or add a spoonful to the plate. Scatter the cabbage over the top and garnish with pea shoots. Drizzle some honey mustard sauce over and put the rest in a sauce pot or boat.

MasterChef highlights and lowlights?

What I truly loved were the professional kitchen rounds when we cooked for and with the Michelin-starred chefs. But I guess the highlight for me was the feedback I got in the Final when John yelped like a cowboy.

My worst moment was nearly chopping my thumb off practising at home. I had to have it stuck back together in hospital. It made me a little cack-handed and slowed me down, especially in the Bond Girls' challenge when I got a bit stressed a nd tearful.

Food Heaven & Hell?

My idea of food heaven would be travelling around Spain and exploring all the regions and their tapas. I have a huge love for Spanish food. It's simple and all about the ingredients.

My idea of food hell is raw celery – it's the devil's food!

BEEF AND OYSTERS SERVES 4

I've tweaked this traditional dish with two interesting ideas: cooking the beef two ways and serving the oysters two ways also. Samphire complements beef really well and, as a seaside plant, is a natural partner for oysters. The rich earthy flavour of the parsley root purée balances the saltiness of the oysters and samphire.

1 x 600g beef fillet
rapeseed oil, for frying
butter, for frying
60g samphire
micro herbs, to garnish

For the braised beef shin
2 tablespoons olive oil
2 carrots, chopped
1 white onion, chopped
2 celery sticks, chopped
1 garlic clove, crushed
2 star anise
5 sprigs of thyme
250ml red wine
250ml Guinness
1 tablespoon honey
500ml beef stock
800g beef shin
a knob of butter

For the oyster emulsion
1 fresh oyster
1 egg yolk
250ml grapeseed oil
a squeeze of lemon juice

For the tempura oysters
4 fresh oysters
oil for deep-frying
50g self-raising flour, plus extra for coating
1 teaspoon baking powder
80ml Guinness
plain flour, for coating

For the parsley root purée
400g parsley root, peeled and chopped
   into even pieces
300ml double cream
150ml milk
salt and pepper to taste

For the braised beef shin. Preheat the oven to 190°C/Gas Mark 5. Heat the olive oil in a flameproof casserole and soften the carrots, onion and celery with the garlic, star anise and thyme. Add the wine and reduce by half, then add the Guinness, honey and stock. Bring to the boil.

Trim any excess fat and sinew from the shin and chop into large chunks. Season them. Sear in some rapeseed oil in a hot frying pan until well browned on all sides. Transfer the beef to the casserole and mix into the Guinness mixture. Place in the oven to cook for 3$^{1}/_{2}$ hours. After this time, check to see if the shin is tender and falling apart. If not, cook for an extra 30 minutes. (Prepare the other elements of the dish while the shin is in the oven.)

When the beef is cooked, remove from the casserole, wrap in foil to keep warm and set aside. Strain the cooking liquid through a fine sieve into a saucepan; discard the vegetables. Bring the liquid to the boil and reduce until thickened. Finish with the butter and season with pepper. Set aside, ready to reheat for serving.

For the oyster emulsion. Remove the oyster from its shell and place in a food processor along with its juices. Add the egg yolk and blitz, slowly adding the oil in a gentle stream. When well blended, add the lemon juice and pepper to taste. Set aside in the fridge.

For the tempura oysters. Remove the oysters from their shells; reserve the oysters in the fridge. Put the shells (top and bottom halves) in a pan of boiling water and boil for 45 minutes to sterilise. Drain and set aside.

For the parsley root purée. Put the parsley root in a saucepan, add the cream and milk and season with salt. Cook for 15-20 minutes or until tender. Using a slotted spoon, transfer the parsley root to a food processor and blitz until smooth (you might need to add

some of the cooking liquid if the purée is too thick). Season with pepper and a little more salt to taste. Keep warm.

For the beef fillet. Portion the beef fillet equally into four steaks. Season with salt and pepper, then drizzle over some rapeseed oil. Heat a frying pan until hot, then add the fillet steaks and cook for 2-3 minutes. Turn the steaks over and add a big knob of butter to the pan. Cook for another 2-3 minutes, basting the steaks with the melted foaming butter (the meat will be medium-rare). Remove from the pan and leave to rest for 5-6 minutes before slicing. Finish the tempura oysters and the samphire while the beef is resting.

To finish the tempura oysters. Heat oil for deep-frying to 180°C. Mix the self-raising flour with the baking powder in a bowl and whisk in the Guinness to make a batter. Dust the oysters with a little plain flour, then coat in the batter, shaking off any excess. Fry in the hot oil for 1-2 minutes or until golden and crisp. Remove and drain on kitchen paper. Keep hot.

For the samphire. Melt a knob of butter in a saucepan, add the samphire and cook for 1 minute or until just tender. Remove from the heat.

To serve. Put a good spoonful of parsley root purée on the left side of each plate. Place some braised beef shin on the purée and alongside it a sliced fillet steak. Next to that place the bottom of an oyster shell on a little samphire. Put a tempura oyster inside the shell and put on the lid, so it is slightly open to reveal the tempura oyster inside. Scatter more samphire next to the oyster. Spoon the reduced cooking liquor on the braised shin and around the plate, along with a little oyster emulsion. Garnish with micro herbs.

PAN-ROASTED DUCK BREAST
WITH MINI FONDANT POTATOES, CARROT AND CUMIN PURÉE
AND A RED PORT JUS SERVES 4

This is what I cooked to get through to the Quarter-Finals. It's a tweaked version of a dish I often cook for friends. I added cumin to the carrots, which gives them a subtle spicing, with micro herbs and pea shoots to add a nice freshness. It's a good dish, but it showed that I had a long way to go to improve in the competition because it's very 'home cooking'.

For the fondant potatoes
4 even-sized large Desiree potatoes
a large knob of unsalted butter
1 tablespoon olive oil
1 sprig of thyme
1 large garlic clove, crushed
250ml chicken stock (or duck stock if you have it)

For the carrot and cumin purée
4 carrots, cut into 2cm pieces
4 tablespoons olive oil
a pinch of ground cumin

For the duck breasts
4 large duck breasts
4 garlic cloves (unpeeled), crushed
4 sprigs of thyme

For the red port jus
100ml port
3 tablespoons redcurrant jelly
2 shallots, roughly chopped
2 sprigs of thyme
2 garlic cloves, crushed
200ml chicken stock
25g unsalted butter, cut into small pieces
salt and pepper to taste

To garnish
growing pea shoots
micro red amaranth

For the fondant potatoes. Preheat the oven to 200°C/Gas Mark 6. Peel the potatoes and cut out two cylinders from each one using a 5cm metal cutter (you want eight cylinders in total). Neaten the top and bottom with a knife so they are flat.

Heat an ovenproof frying pan and melt the butter with the oil. Add the potatoes and colour them all over – top and bottom and on the sides; use tongs to turn them. Add the thyme, garlic and stock to the pan. Cover with a cartouche (a circle of buttered greaseproof paper that will cover the pan completely) and transfer to the oven. Cook for 40-45 minutes or until the potatoes are soft and cooked through; halfway through the cooking, baste the potatoes with the stock so the tops don't dry out (then replace the cartouche). Make the other elements of the dish while the potatoes are in the oven.

For the carrot and cumin purée. Cook the carrots in a pan of boiling water until tender. Drain and place in a blender with the olive oil, cumin and some salt and pepper. Blend for 4-5 minutes or until very smooth. Spoon into a saucepan and set aside, ready to reheat for serving.

For the duck breasts. Score the skin on the duck breasts, without cutting into the flesh. Season both sides of each breast. Place the breasts skin side down in a cold non-stick frying pan (starting in a cold pan will render the fat slowly). Set on the heat and cook for 4-5 minutes or until the skin has a good colour and is crisp.

Add the garlic cloves and thyme and turn the breasts over. Reduce the heat and cook for 4-5 minutes. Turn the breasts on to the skin side again and cook for 3 minutes. Turn over and cook for another 3 minutes, then turn once more and cook on the skin side for a final 2 minutes. The total cooking time will be 18 minutes. Remove the duck breasts from the pan and leave to rest in a warm place for 5-7 minutes while you make the jus.

For the red port jus. Remove the garlic and thyme from pan (discard these) and skim off excess fat. Deglaze the frying pan with the port, then add the redcurrant jelly and whisk until melted. Add the shallots, thyme sprigs, garlic and stock to the pan. Bring to the boil and reduce by half. Pass through a sieve into a saucepan. Gradually whisk in the butter and season to taste. Keep warm.

To serve. Make a line of carrot purée on each plate. Cut each duck breast into four slices and arrange in a criss-cross line on the other side of the plate, with a fondant potato at each end. Drizzle a little jus over the duck and garnish with some pea shoots. Garnish the carrot purée with red amaranth.

PAN-ROASTED PIGEON WITH ORANGE BRAISED LENTILS, CHICORY AND HAZELNUTS SERVES 4

Pigeon isn't everyone's cup of tea, but when I ate it at Heston's six months earlier, I liked it. Pigeon has to be served rare because if overcooked it tastes like liver. As it's such a small bird I cooked it on the bone to keep it moist. All game needs something sweet, so I used orange balsamic in the dressing and lentils. The chicory brings some crunch and a bitterness to cut through the sweetness and balance the dish. Chargrilling the chicory and dressing it with a little balsamic tones down the bitterness perfectly.

25g blanched (skinned) hazelnuts
3 oven-ready wood pigeons
Maldon sea salt
3 bay leaves
6 sprigs of thyme
6 pieces of orange peel
3 tablespoons olive oil, plus extra for
    drizzling
micro parsley, to garnish

For the celeriac purée
300g celeriac, peeled, cut into 2cm chunks
250ml double cream

For the lentils
1 tablespoon olive oil
80g smoked bacon lardons
2 tablespoons finely diced shallot
1 tablespoon diced orange carrot
1 tablespoon diced yellow carrot
2 tablespoons diced celery
2 bay leaves
picked leaves from 6 sprigs of thyme
2 pieces of orange peel
100g Puy lentils, rinsed well
about 500ml white chicken stock
grated zest of 1/2 orange
about 2 tablespoons orange balsamic
    vinegar, to taste
4 tablespoons chopped flat-leaf parsley

For the dressing
2 tablespoons groundnut oil
2 tablespoons hazelnut oil
2 tablespoons orange balsamic vinegar

For the chicory
1 red chicory (you need 8 leaves)
1 white chicory (you need 8 leaves)
olive oil
orange balsamic vinegar, for dressing
salt and pepper to taste

For the celeriac purée. Put the celeriac into a saucepan with the cream, 100ml water and some salt. Bring to the boil, then simmer on a very low heat for 25–30 minutes or until tender; stir every 5 minutes to ensure the cream doesn't catch on the bottom of the pan. Using a slotted spoon, transfer the celeriac to a food processor and blitz until smooth, adding a little of the cooking liquor if needed. Season to taste. Set aside in a pan, ready to reheat for serving.

For the lentils. Heat the olive oil in a saucepan, add the bacon lardons and cook until they start to brown. Add the shallot, carrots and celery and cook until softened. Add the bay leaves, thyme, orange peel and lentils and cook for 1 minute, then pour in enough stock to come 2cm above the surface of the lentils. Bring to the boil, then reduce the heat and simmer for 25–30 minutes or until the lentils are tender and have absorbed the stock.

Discard the orange peel and bay leaves. Season the lentils with salt and pepper and add the grated orange zest. Stir in 2 tablespoons balsamic vinegar and the parsley. Taste the lentils to see if you need to add more vinegar. Keep warm, or reheat for serving. (While the lentils are cooking you can make the dressing and toast the hazelnuts.)

For the dressing. Put all the dressing ingredients in a bowl and whisk well to mix. Season with a pinch of salt. Set aside.

For the hazelnuts. Preheat the oven to 190°C/Gas Mark 5. Spread the nuts on a small baking tray and toast for 3–5 minutes or until lightly browned. Tip into a mortar and lightly crush with the pestle, keeping the nuts in rough chunks. Set aside. Leave the oven on.

For the pigeons. Remove the wings, legs and wishbone from each pigeon. (You could keep these to make stock, or freeze them to make a stock at a later date.) Season the cavity in each bird with Maldon salt and pepper, then stuff with a bay leaf, 2 sprigs of thyme and 2 pieces of orange peel. Drizzle with a little olive oil and season the breasts with salt.

Heat the olive oil in an ovenproof frying pan and sear the pigeons on all sides until golden brown. Transfer the pan to the oven and roast for 5-7 minutes or until plump (the birds are to be served rare; if you overcook them they will taste liver-ish). Lift the birds on to a carving board and leave to rest for 10 minutes, then remove the breasts using a small paring knife. Cut each breast on the diagonal into two pieces.

For the chicory. Prepare the chicory while the pigeons are resting. Discard any damaged outer leaves from the red and white chicory, then separate the remaining leaves. You will need four leaves for each serving (two red and two white). Drizzle these with olive oil and season with salt. Heat a ridged griddle pan and cook the leaves for 30 seconds on each side or until tender. Drizzle with a little orange balsamic and season with pepper.

To serve. Make a teardrop shape of celeriac purée on the left hand side of each plate. Make a well in the purée for the lentils to rest in, then spoon the lentils on to the purée. Fold the chicory leaves in half and place on the lentils. Arrange three pieces of pigeon on the chicory in a line, then scatter the hazelnuts over the top and drizzle with the dressing. Garnish with micro parsley.

Making Pan-roasted Pigeon with Orange Braised Lentils, Chicory and Hazelnuts, (see page 52)

QUAIL BALLOTINE, QUAIL LEG CONFIT, CRISP QUAIL'S EGG, WILD MUSHROOMS AND A QUAIL JUS

SERVES 4

FROM THE SERIES

When we cooked for the Bond Girls we were told to create an exceptional dish suitable for fine dining. I was given the starter course, which needed to be dainty, elegant and a good opening for the dinner. In devising this dish I had to teach myself new techniques like making a ballotine and confit. The flavours are a classic combination, but the preparation on the day pushed me to the limits as there are so many elements. Finishing the egg and mushrooms with truffle salt/oil enhances their flavours really well, but dress lightly otherwise the truffle will overpower the whole dish.

4 quails
unsalted butter, for finishing confit, ballotines and jus
200ml red wine

For the quail stock
olive oil, for frying
1 onion, roughly chopped
2 carrots, roughly chopped
1 celery stick, roughly chopped
1 leek, roughly chopped
500ml chicken stock
10 black peppercorns
2 bay leaves and 4 sprigs of parsley

For the chicken mousse
150g mixed wild mushrooms (e.g. girolles, enoki, black trumpets), chopped
1 shallot, finely chopped
olive oil, for frying
2 tablespoons chopped parsley
leaves picked from 2 sprigs of thyme
1 large skinless, boneless chicken breast, diced
50ml single cream
2 egg whites

For the quail leg confit
leaves picked from 2 sprigs of thyme
250ml duck fat

For the crisp quail's eggs
4 quail's eggs
3 tablespoons white wine vinegar
oil for deep-frying
truffle salt

For the parsnip purée
4 large parsnips, diced
250ml chicken stock
250ml milk

For the wild mushrooms
1 tablespoon finely chopped shallot
a knob of unsalted butter
50g mixed wild mushrooms (buna shimeji, girolles or chanterelles, golden enoki, black trumpets)
1 tablespoon chopped parsley
white truffle oil
salt and pepper to taste

To garnish
micro cress and red amaranth

For the quails. Remove the wings and legs from the quails; reserve four of the legs for the confit and the remaining legs plus the wings for the stock. Using sturdy scissors, split open each quail down the back, as you would when spatchcocking a chicken, then press open. Carefully cut away the carcass to leave the two breasts still attached to each other, with their skin. Reserve the carcasses for the stock. Set aside the four butterflied boneless breasts and the four legs for the confit in the fridge.

For the quail stock. Chop up the quail carcasses. Heat a little olive oil in a large stock pot and brown the chopped carcasses with the remaining four legs

and the wings. Add the onion, carrots, celery and leek and cook until softened and lightly browned. Pour in the chicken stock and about 500ml of water – the ingredients in the pot should be covered with liquid. Add the peppercorns, bay leaves and parsley. Bring to the boil, then simmer for 1 1/2 hours, skimming off any fat and scum that rises to the top. Pass through a sieve into a bowl or jug and reserve for the jus. (Any stock not used for the jus can be frozen and kept for other quail or poultry sauces.) Make the mousse, confit and ballotines while the stock is simmering.

For the chicken mousse. Fry the mushrooms and shallot in a pan with a little olive oil. Add the herbs and remove from the heat. Put the chicken breast in a food processor and turn on the machine, slowly adding the cream through the feed tube. Add the mushroom and shallot mixture and keep blitzing until smooth. Pass through a drum sieve into a bowl, to remove any gristle.

In a separate bowl, whisk the egg whites until stiff. Fold into the chicken mixture and season with salt and pepper. Spoon the mousse into a piping bag fitted with a small tube. Keep in the fridge until needed.

continued on page 58

continued from page 57

For the quail leg confit. Preheat the oven to 160°C/Gas Mark 3. Remove the thigh bone from the four quail legs; push the thigh meat up and tuck into the leg meat. Season with salt and pepper. Lay the legs in a small roasting tray. Sprinkle with the thyme leaves and cover with duck fat. Cook in the oven for 35-45 minutes or until soft, turning the legs every 15 minutes. Lift out the quail legs and leave to drain on kitchen paper. Before serving, reheat in a saucepan with a little butter.

For the quail's eggs. Gently place the quail's eggs in a pan of boiling water and cook for 2 minutes. Remove and plunge into a bowl of iced water mixed with the vinegar (this will help to loosen the shells). Leave for 1 hour so they will be easier to peel.

For the quail ballotines. Lay out each butterflied quail, skin side down, on a sheet of clingfilm. Season with salt and pepper. Pipe the chicken mousse down the middle of a butterflied quail, then roll up the quail around the mousse into a cylinder, using the clingfilm to help. Roll the ballotine again in clingfilm. Twist the ends tightly and tie with string to keep in place. Make the remaining three ballotines in the same way, then set aside in the fridge for 30 minutes to firm up.

Poach the ballotines in a pan of simmering water for 25-30 minutes. Lift out and leave to rest for 5 minutes, then remove from the clingfilm. Before serving, finish by colouring on all sides in a pan with a little butter. (Make the parsnip purée and jus while the ballotines are being poached.)

For the parsnip purée. Put the parsnips in a saucepan, cover with the stock and milk and season with salt. Bring to the boil, then simmer until tender. Using a slotted spoon, transfer the parsnips to a food processor and blitz for about 5 minutes or until very smooth, adding some of the cooking liquid if the purée is too thick. Season with salt and pepper to taste. Put into a saucepan and set aside, ready to reheat for serving.

For the quail jus. Pour the red wine into a wide pan and boil to reduce by half. Add 500ml of the quail stock and continue boiling until the liquid has reduced by half. Strain through a fine sieve into a clean pan. Check the seasoning and adjust to taste. Add a large knob of butter and set aside, ready to reheat for serving.

For the crisp quail's eggs. Heat oil for deep-frying to 180°C. Peel the eggs, then dry well on kitchen paper. Deep-fry for about 30 seconds. Drain on kitchen paper, then season with truffle salt. Keep hot.

For the wild mushrooms. Soften the shallot in the butter in a pan. Add the mushrooms and sauté for 2 minutes. Add the parsley and stir well, then remove from the heat. Drizzle a little truffle oil over the mushrooms.

To serve. For each plate, at 2 o'clock put a small spoonful of the parsnip purée. Cut each ballotine in half on the diagonal and set cut side up next to the purée. Put the crisp quail's egg at 11 o'clock, and place three mushrooms along the bottom of the ballotine. Set the confit leg at 7 o'clock. Garnish with micro cress and red amaranth. Drizzle a little jus on the ballotine and around the plate.

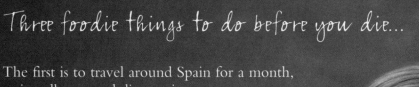

Three foodie things to do before you die...

The first is to travel around Spain for a month, eating all over and discovering new tastes.

Second is to cook for the Queen.

And third, to open my own restaurant in the East End, staying true to my roots.

VENISON WITH DUKKAH, BUTTERNUT SQUASH PURÉE & SPICED POMEGRANATE PEARL BARLEY

SERVES 4

I was watching *Saturday Kitchen* one morning, and the chef was making dukkah.
I'd never seen it before and it looked really exciting. After some research I learned that
it is Moroccan/Middle Eastern. It adds an exotic touch to this dish. I think that the
sweetness from the pomegranate and the toasty hazelnut flavour go really well with it.
The squash purée and pearl barley add interesting textures to complete the dish.

4 pieces of venison fillet, about 200g each
rapeseed oil, for frying
micro coriander, to garnish

For the dukkah mix
50g blanched (skinned) hazelnuts
1 tablespoon sesame seeds
1 tablespoon nigella seeds
1 tablespoon desiccated coconut
1 tablespoon coriander seeds
1 teaspoon cumin seeds

For the squash purée
1 medium butternut squash
rapeseed oil
salt and pepper to taste

For the pearl barley
1 onion, diced
1 carrot, diced
1 celery stick, diced
1 tablespoon rapeseed oil
1/2 teaspoon coriander seeds
1/2 teaspoon cumin seeds
180g pearl barley, soaked overnight in
    water and drained
2 strips of orange peel
300ml chicken stock
2 tablespoons chopped flat-leaf parsley
2 tablespoons finely chopped coriander
2 tablespoons pomegranate molasses
seeds and juice from 1 pomegranate
salt and pepper to taste

For the dukkah mix. Toast the hazelnuts in a dry pan for 1-2 minutes, then add the remaining ingredients and toast for 1 more minute on a gentle heat. Cool slightly, then tip into a spice grinder and pulse to a fine powder (or use a pestle and mortar). Set aside.

For the squash purée. Preheat the oven to 190°C/Gas Mark 5. Cut the squash lengthways in half and scoop out the seeds. Place cut side up in a baking tray. Drizzle over some rapeseed oil and sprinkle with salt. Bake for 45-60 minutes or until softened.

Scoop out the flesh and place in a food processor. Add a good glug of rapeseed oil and some pepper and blitz to a smooth purée. Check the seasoning and add more salt if needed. Set aside in a pan, ready to reheat for serving. Leave the oven on for the venison.

For the pearl barley. You can cook the barley while the squash is in the oven. Soften the onion, carrot and celery in the rapeseed oil in a saucepan. Grind the coriander and cumin seeds in a pestle and mortar, then add to the vegetables along with the pearl barley and orange peel. Stir to mix. Pour in the chicken stock and add half the chopped parsley and coriander and the pomegranate molasses. Bring to the boil, then reduce the heat and simmer for 25-30 minutes or until the pearl barley is tender.

Add the remaining chopped herbs, the pomegranate juice and half the pomegranate seeds. Season with salt and pepper. Set aside, ready to reheat for serving.

For the venison. Season the venison with salt and pepper and rub with a little rapeseed oil. Heat a large ovenproof frying pan and sear the venison on both sides, then transfer to the oven. Roast for 8 minutes. Remove from the oven and leave to rest for 10 minutes before slicing.

To serve. Make a line of squash purée in the middle of each plate and spoon the pearl barley on the squash. Lay the slices of venison on the pearl barley. Sprinkle each serving with a teaspoon of dukkah, then garnish with pomegranate seeds and micro coriander.

RABBIT LOIN WRAPPED IN SERRANO HAM
WITH COCKLES, CAULIFLOWER PURÉE, SAMPHIRE AND
A COCKLE VINAIGRETTE   SERVES 4

This dish was inspired by a holiday in Malta, where there is a lot of rabbit and seafood on restaurant menus. The Spanish use rabbit and seafood in paellas so I knew they worked together, but I wanted to adapt them to my style of cooking. I added the ham for its flavour as well as to keep the rabbit moist, and creamy cauliflower, which worked really well with similar ingredients when I was with Adam Byatt at Trinity. I am a big fan of pairing things that grow together so I added some samphire. As the cauliflower purée is very rich and the dish has a slight game flavour, a vinaigrette provided the acidity needed to balance the plate.

4 large rabbit loins
olive oil
8 slices of good-quality Serrano ham
salt and pepper to taste

For the cauliflower purée
1 cauliflower, finely chopped
300ml milk
300ml double cream

For the cockles and samphire
400g cockles
3 tablespoons plain flour
100g samphire

For the cockle vinaigrette
8 tablespoons olive oil
4 tablespoons cider vinegar
½ shallot, finely chopped
2 tablespoons finely chopped dill leaves
a squeeze of lemon juice

For the cauliflower purée. Put the cauliflower in a saucepan and cover with the milk and cream. Add a pinch of salt. Bring to the boil, then simmer for 10 minutes or until tender. Drain, reserving the cooking liquid, and tip into a food processor. Blitz for 4-5 minutes or until very smooth, adding some of the cooking liquid if the purée is too thick. Season with pepper and a little more salt to taste. Set aside in a saucepan, ready to reheat for serving.

For the cockles and samphire. Put the cockles in a bowl of water with the flour (it will draw out the grit) and leave for at least an hour before cooking. Drain the cockles.

Heat a deep pan and add the cockles and samphire (you do not need to add any water). Cover with a lid and steam for 3-5 minutes or until the cockle shells open. Strain the juices through a fine sieve into a bowl and reserve for the vinaigrette. Tip the cockles and samphire into another bowl. Leave 12 cockles in shell and pick the rest from their shells. Set aside.

For the cockle vinaigrette. Whisk together the olive oil and cider vinegar in a small bowl. In a separate bowl mix together the shallot, dill and 25ml strained cockle juice. Gradually whisk

in the oil/vinegar mixture, tasting as you go. You may not need all the oil/vinegar mixture or want to add more of the cockle juice. Add the lemon juice and a little pinch of salt. Set aside.

For the rabbit loin. Preheat the oven to 180°C/Gas Mark 4. Season the loins with a tiny bit of salt and a good grind of pepper and drizzle with a little olive oil. Roll each loin in two slices of Serrano ham. Heat an ovenproof frying pan with some olive oil and fry the rabbit loins for 1-2 minutes, just to colour the ham all over. Transfer the pan to the oven to cook for 7-10 minutes. Remove from the oven and lift the rabbit loins on to a plate. Pour the juices from the pan over the rabbit, cover with foil and leave to rest for 4-5 minutes before cutting each loin into three pieces.

To serve. On each plate, put a spoonful of cauliflower purée at 12, 4 and 8 o'clock. Next to each spoonful place a piece of the rabbit (three pieces on each plate). Put two cockles out of shell and one cockle in shell next to each slice of rabbit. Scatter the samphire over the rabbit/cockles and drizzle with the vinaigrette.

Rabbit is a very underused meat
but it tastes amazing and is great value.

Making Rabbit Loin Wrapped in Serrano Ham with Cockles, Cauliflower Purée, Samphire and a Cockle Vinaigrette (see page 62).

MASTERCHEF | THE FINALISTS COOKBOOK

CHOCOLATE AND HAZELNUT CRUMBLE TART

WITH RIPPLED CHANTILLY CREAM AND RASPBERRY COULIS   MAKES 4 TARTS

This dessert came from flavours that I like to eat together – I think chocolate and raspberries complement each other, as do hazelnuts and chocolate. I put the crumble on top for texture but also to incorporate the hazelnuts into the dessert. Cream flavoured with vanilla softens the rich, bittersweet dark chocolate filling of the tart.

For the pastry
250g plain flour
a pinch of salt
110g unsalted butter, cut into cubes
100g caster sugar
1 egg yolk, beaten, for brushing

For the chocolate filling
185g dark chocolate (about 70% cocoa solids), broken into pieces
185ml double cream
4 egg yolks

For the hazelnut crumble topping
60g blanched (skinned) hazelnuts
75g plain flour
60g unsalted butter
60g golden caster sugar
icing sugar, for dusting

For the raspberry coulis
200g raspberries
2 tablespoons icing sugar
1 tablespoon lemon juice

For the rippled Chantilly cream
150ml double cream
2 tablespoons icing sugar
seeds from 1 vanilla pod

For the pastry. Put the flour, salt and butter into a food processor and blitz until the mixture is like breadcrumbs. Add the sugar and pulse to mix. Gradually add 6 tablespoons of cold water to make a dough. Shape into a ball, wrap in clingfilm and leave to rest in the fridge for at least 30 minutes.

Divide the pastry into four equal portions. Roll out each portion thinly on a floured work surface. Use to line four loose-bottomed 10cm fluted tart tins. Rest in the fridge for at least 30 minutes.

Preheat the oven to 180°C/Gas Mark 4. Prick the bottom of each pastry case with a fork, then line with a circle of baking parchment and fill with baking beans. Set the tins on a baking tray and bake blind for 10 minutes. Remove the beans and paper, then return to the oven to bake for a further 10 minutes or until the pastry is cooked. Allow to cool slightly before brushing with beaten egg yolk to seal. Set aside. Leave the oven on.

For the chocolate filling. Put the chocolate and cream in a heatproof bowl, set over a saucepan of gently simmering water and melt gently, stirring occasionally. Remove the bowl from the pan and leave to cool a little, then mix in the egg yolks, one at a time. Divide the chocolate mix among the cooked tart cases. Bake for 3-5 minutes or until the filling has softly set.

Remove from the oven (leave it on) and allow to cool, then set aside in the fridge.

For the hazelnut crumble topping. Blitz the hazelnuts in a food processor to a fine crumb. Tip into a mixing bowl. Blitz the flour and butter together in the processor until the mixture resembles breadcrumbs. Add to the hazelnuts along with the caster sugar and mix together. Spread out on a baking tray and bake for 15-20 minutes or until golden brown; halfway through the cooking, stir the crumble to be sure it isn't sticking or burning. Leave to cool, then sprinkle over the top of each tart and finish with a dusting of icing sugar.

For the raspberry coulis. Put all the ingredients in a blender or food processor and blitz until smooth, then pass through a sieve into a bowl or jug, to remove the seeds.

For the rippled Chantilly cream. Whip the cream with the icing sugar and vanilla seeds to soft peaks. Fold 2-3 tablespoons of the raspberry coulis through the cream to create a rippled effect. Keep in a cool place until ready to serve.

To serve. Place a small spoonful of cream underneath each tart, to prevent it from sliding around the plate. Add a quenelle of rippled Chantilly cream to the plate and the raspberry coulis in a small pouring pot.

COCONUT RICE PUDDING WITH BLUEBERRY COMPOTE AND MACADAMIA NUTS SERVES 4

Everybody loves rice pudding, don't they? Well in my family we do. I thought I would try some different flavours to pimp up the traditional rice pudding, and think that the coconut milk here works well with the blueberries, and macadamia nuts add an extra nutty richness. There are many different variations you can make, so depending on your mood you can adapt the basic recipe to your taste.

200g pudding rice
300ml whole milk
80g caster sugar
1 x 400ml can coconut milk
1 vanilla pod, split open
50g macadamia nuts
20g desiccated coconut
fine strips of orange zest, to garnish

For the blueberry compote
250g blueberries
1 tablespoon caster sugar
2 strips of orange peel

For the rice pudding. Put the rice, milk, caster sugar and coconut milk in a saucepan. Scrape the seeds from the vanilla pod and add to the pan along with the pod. Cook gently for about 20 minutes or until the rice has softened; stir every few minutes so the rice doesn't catch on the bottom of the pan. When the rice is ready, remove from the heat and keep warm. (While the rice pudding is cooking, prepare the other elements of the dish.)

For the blueberry compote. Reserve a few of the blueberries for garnish and put the rest in a saucepan with the caster sugar and orange peel. Heat for 2-4 minutes or until the blueberries start to release their juices and become jam-like. Remove the orange peel and set the compote aside until ready to serve.

For the macadamia nuts. Toast the nuts in a frying pan, then pulse in a food processor until roughly chopped. Set aside.

For the toasted coconut. Toast the desiccated coconut in the frying pan for about 20 seconds, keeping a close eye on it as it can burn quickly. Tip on to a plate and leave to cool.

To serve. Spoon a layer of rice pudding into each serving glass, then add a layer of blueberry compote. Add another layer of rice, followed by a layer of compote and a final layer of rice. Top with toasted coconut, macadamia nuts, the reserved whole blueberries and orange zest. This is best served warm, although you could also serve it cold.

You can adapt the basic recipe
with flavours that suit your tastes.

FIG AND FRANGIPANE TART WITH AN ORANGE MASCARPONE CREAM SERVES 4

FROM THE SERIES

I cooked this dessert for the critics. I was going to cook a fondant, but as I did that in the invention test for Marcus Wareing, I changed my dessert at the last minute. Figs were in season so I thought they would be a great starting point. Almonds and oranges complement figs well so I took a classic route to make mini tartlets.

4 figs, cut vertically into quarters
icing sugar, for dusting
grated orange zest, to garnish

For the pastry
250g plain flour
50g icing sugar
125g unsalted butter, diced
1 egg, beaten

For the frangipane
100g unsalted butter, softened
100g caster sugar
1 egg
100g ground almonds

For the orange mascarpone cream
150ml double cream
250g mascarpone
2 tablespoons icing sugar
grated zest of 1 orange, or to taste
2 tablespoons Cointreau, or to taste

For the pastry. Sift the flour and icing sugar together, then tip into a food processor. Add the butter and pulse until you have a breadcrumb consistency. Add the egg and pulse until the mixture comes together to make a dough. Form into a ball, wrap in clingfilm and chill for at least 30 minutes.

Preheat the oven to 180°C/Gas Mark 4. Roll out the dough thinly on a lightly floured surface and use to line four loose-bottomed 10cm fluted flan tins. If you have the time, place the pastry cases in the fridge to rest and firm up for 30 minutes. When ready to bake, prick the bottom of each case with a fork, line with a circle of baking parchment and fill with baking beans. Set the tins on a baking tray and bake blind for 10 minutes. Remove the paper and baking beans, then return to the oven and bake for a further 5-10 minutes or until a light golden colour. You don't want to cook the pastry completely as it will be baked further, with the filling. Allow to cool. Leave the oven on.

For the frangipane. Blend the butter with the sugar in a food processor. With the machine running, gradually add the egg and ground almonds and blitz to a paste. Transfer to a bowl, cover and chill for 20 minutes.

For the orange mascarpone cream. While the frangipane is chilling, whisk together the cream, mascarpone, icing sugar, and orange zest and Cointreau to taste until smooth. Keep in the fridge until needed.

To finish the tarts. Divide the frangipane among the tart cases, smoothing it out. Arrange the fig quarters on top and dust with icing sugar. Bake for 25-30 minutes or until the frangipane is golden brown and firm on the surface (it will be slightly soft inside). Remove from the oven and dust with a little more icing sugar.

To serve. Place a dot of the cream off-centre on each plate and set a tart on it. Add a quenelle of orange mascarpone cream next to the tart. Grate a little orange zest over the plate to garnish. (Any leftover cream would go well with fresh figs and crushed almonds as a tasty treat.)

GREEK HONEY FROZEN YOGHURT WITH PISTACHIO MERINGUE, CARAMELISED SHARON FRUIT AND BLACKBERRY SAUCE

SERVES 4

Every day on the way to and from work I pop into my local shop. The man who owns the shop – 'Boss' – was eating a sharon fruit one day. He cut me a piece off to taste. When I got home I looked online to see what sorts of flavours complement sharon fruit and saw that it is a Greek/Mediterranean fruit. So that made me think of yoghurt instead of ice cream, and lemon and honey to sweeten. I wanted to add nuts to the recipe, so used them in the meringue to give a unique texture.

For the frozen yoghurt
500g Greek-style yoghurt
5 tablespoons Greek runny honey
2 teaspoons vanilla paste
juice of 1/2 lemon

For the pistachio meringue
30g shelled pistachios
2 egg whites
75g caster sugar
1/2 teaspoon white wine vinegar

For the sharon fruit
2 sharon fruits
5 tablespoons caster sugar

For the blackberry sauce
100g blackberries
juice of 1/2 lemon
1 tablespoon icing sugar

ground toasted pistachios, to garnish

For the frozen yoghurt. Mix together all the ingredients in a bowl or a jug. Pour into an ice cream machine and churn according to the manufacturer's instructions. This should take around 30 minutes, depending on the machine. Once churned to the consistency of ice cream, transfer to a freezer container and keep in the freezer until ready to serve. (If made ahead and frozen hard, leave to soften at room temperature for 5 minutes before serving.)

For the pistachio meringue. Preheat the oven to 160°C/Gas Mark 3. Blitz the pistachios in a spice grinder or mini food processor until finely ground. Set aside. Whisk the egg whites with an electric mixer to stiff peaks. Add the sugar, 1 tablespoon at a time, whisking well between each addition. Fold in the vinegar and pistachios using a spatula or large metal spoon. Spoon the meringue mixture on to a baking tray lined with greaseproof paper or baking parchment and spread out into a layer about 5mm thick. Reduce the oven temperature to 150°C/Gas Mark 2 and bake the meringue for 45 minutes or until the outside is set; the inside will be chewy. Leave to cool on the baking tray. Once cool, smash into fragments or shards and set aside.

For the sharon fruit. Cut each fruit into six wedges. Put the caster sugar on a plate and roll the fruit in the sugar to coat. Heat a ridged griddle pan, then cook the sharon fruit for 2 minutes on each side or until caramelised. Remove from the pan and set aside.

For the blackberry sauce. Put the blackberries, lemon juice and icing sugar into a bowl and blend with a hand blender until smooth. Pass the mixture through a sieve to remove the seeds.

To serve. Place a big scoop of frozen yoghurt in the middle of each bowl or plate and surround with the caramelised sharon fruit and meringue shards. Drizzle over the blackberry sauce and garnish with a sprinkling of ground pistachios.

Inspired by the flavours of Greece!

MILK ICE CREAM WITH HONEYCOMB PIECES, PICKLED BLACKBERRIES, BLACKBERRY GEL, LAVENDER FLOWERS AND HAZELNUT DUST   SERVES 4

Desserts have never been my strong point, so I wanted to try creating something new, thinking outside the box. My first thought was milk ice cream, which brings back childhood memories of milk ice lollies. The next thing that came to me was fruit. Blackberries were in season at the time and I thought they would complement the ice cream. While shopping in Borough Market I picked up a jar of orange Greek honey, which I decided to use to make honeycomb. At the next stall I saw dandelion and burdock and thought of pickling the blackberries with it. It all came together in this dish, which I cooked for the artists in the castle when we were in Italy.

For the ice cream
800ml whole milk
80g caster sugar
100ml condensed milk
20g liquid glucose
1 gelatine leaf

For the honeycomb
200g caster sugar
70g liquid glucose
35g orange blossom honey
1 tablespoon bicarbonate of soda

For the blackberry gel
120g blackberries
a squeeze of lemon juice
2 tablespoons icing sugar
1 gelatine leaf
60g caster sugar
1g agar agar

For the pickled blackberries
100g caster sugar
40ml dandelion and burdock drink
100ml white wine vinegar
12 blackberries

To garnish
50g blanched (skinned) hazelnuts
lavender flowers

For the ice cream. Put 750ml of the milk in a large saucepan, add the sugar and heat gently until the sugar has dissolved. Increase the heat and simmer, stirring regularly, until reduced to 500ml. Reduce the heat to low again and add the condensed milk and glucose. Stir until incorporated and smooth, then remove from the heat.

While the milk is simmering, soak the gelatine in cold water for about 10 minutes to soften. Squeeze the gelatine to remove excess water, then add to the warm milk mix and stir until melted. Add the remaining 50ml milk and mix in. Leave to cool, then pour into an ice cream machine and churn according to the manufacturer's instructions. Once churned to the consistency of ice cream, transfer to a freezer container and keep in the freezer until ready to serve. (If you make the ice cream in advance and it is too firm, take it out of the freezer 5 minutes before serving so it can soften a bit.)

For the honeycomb. Put the sugar, glucose, honey and 3 tablespoons water into a large heavy-based pan and cook over a medium heat, stirring occasionally, until a golden caramel is formed. Add the bicarbonate of soda and mix in well (the honeycomb will expand rapidly), then tip into a deep baking tray lined with baking parchment. Leave to cool and set. Once cold, bash the honeycomb into pieces and set aside until needed.

For the blackberry gel. Put the blackberries into a food processor with the lemon juice and icing sugar. Blitz until smooth, then pass through a sieve into a bowl, to remove the pips. Set aside.

Soak the gelatine in cold water for about 10 minutes to soften. Meanwhile, heat the caster sugar with 150ml water in a pan until dissolved, then boil until reduced slightly to a syrup. Squeeze excess water from the gelatine and add to the pan along with the blackberry purée and agar agar. Stir until melted and smooth. Bring back to the boil, then pour into a measuring jug. Cool for 10 minutes, then chill for at least 30 minutes. Before serving, blitz the gel in a mini food processor to slightly loosen it.

For the pickled blackberries. Heat the sugar with the dandelion and burdock drink and vinegar in a pan until dissolved. Bring to the boil and boil for about 5 minutes to reduce a little, then pour into a bowl. Add the blackberries and leave to infuse for about 30 minutes. Remove the blackberries from the liquid using a slotted spoon and set aside.

For the hazelnut dust. Preheat the oven to 180°C/Gas Mark 4. Spread the hazelnuts on a small baking tray and roast for about 4 minutes. Tip into a mini food processor and blitz to a fine crumb.

To serve. Paint each plate with one brush of blackberry gel. Put a scoop of ice cream in the middle. Arrange three pickled blackberries around the ice cream. Add a scattering of honeycomb pieces. Sprinkle with a little hazelnut dust and finish with lavender over the plate.

RASPBERRY SOUFFLÉ WITH PEACH ICE CREAM

SERVES 2

For my first (unsuccessful) audition with *MasterChef* I made a twist on classic Peach Melba, which was invented in 1892 by Auguste Escoffier at the Savoy Hotel (where I cooked for the Bond Girls), and named for Nellie Melba, an Australian soprano. When I finally made it on to *MasterChef* I decided to devise another dessert based on the flavour combo of Peach Melba but with a soufflé, raspberries within the soufflé and a peach ice cream. You could always serve the soufflé with vanilla ice cream or have the ice cream on its own. But I like them together!

For the ice cream
250ml double cream
250ml whole milk
6 egg yolks
150g caster sugar
1 tablespoon vanilla paste
3 peaches

For the soufflé
unsalted butter and caster sugar, for the
    moulds
250g raspberries
100g caster sugar
juice of 1/2 lemon
1 teaspoon cornflour
4 egg whites
icing sugar, for dusting

For the ice cream. Heat the cream with the milk in a heavy-based saucepan to 80°C. Whisk together the egg yolks and caster sugar in a mixing bowl. When the creamy mixture has reached temperature, slowly whisk it into the egg yolk mix. Pour back into the pan and gently cook, stirring with a wooden spoon, until the custard thickens enough to coat the back of the spoon. Pass the mixture through a sieve into a bowl and add the vanilla paste. Leave to cool to room temperature.

Peel the peaches and chop into rough chunks. Blitz to a purée in a food processor. Set aside until you are ready to churn the ice cream.

Pour the custard base and the peach purée into your ice cream machine and churn according to the manufacturer's instructions. Transfer to a freezer container and keep in the freezer until ready to serve. (If made ahead and frozen hard, leave the ice cream to soften at room temperature for 5 minutes before serving.)

For the soufflé. Preheat the oven to 180°C/Gas Mark 4. Grease two 125ml ramekins with butter, then sprinkle some sugar inside and tip the mould so the bottom and sides are coated. Set aside.

Put the raspberries, 50g of the caster sugar and the lemon juice in a bowl and blitz with a hand blender to make a purée. Pass through a sieve into a pan, to remove any seeds. Mix the cornflour with a few drops of water, then add to the raspberry purée in the pan. Heat, stirring, to thicken. Remove from the heat and spoon a tablespoon of the purée into each ramekin.

Whisk the egg whites in a mixing bowl to stiff peaks. Whisk in the remaining caster sugar a tablespoon at a time. Fold a third of the whisked whites into the rest of the raspberry purée, then gently and gradually fold in the remaining whites – you don't want to knock the air out of the mixture. Divide between the ramekins. Set them on a baking tray and bake for 12-15 minutes or until risen and set.

To serve. Dust the soufflés with icing sugar and serve each on a plate with a scoop of ice cream.

I love the flavour combination of vanilla, raspberry and peaches.

CHOCOLATE PANNACOTTA WITH CARAMELISED PEARS AND HAZELNUT BISCUITS SERVES 4

Whenever I have family and friends over for dinner I serve up pannacotta. Everyone thinks it is really hard to make, but it isn't. The only thing you have to get right is to be sure it has a good wobble – you don't want it to set firm. Chocolate and hazelnuts are a marriage made in heaven, so I flavoured the pannacotta with chocolate and made biscuits with hazelnuts. Pears have a clean, juicy sweetness that works really well with the nutty biscuits and chocolate. All flavours I love to eat.

For the chocolate decoration
150g plain chocolate (about 70% cocoa solids), broken into pieces

For the pannacotta
250ml double cream
250ml whole milk
50g caster sugar
2 tablespoons cocoa powder
seeds from 1 vanilla pod
3 gelatine leaves

For the caramelised pears
2 ripe but firm Williams pears
100g golden caster sugar

For the hazelnut biscuits
90g blanched (skinned) hazelnuts
130g unsalted butter
75g golden caster sugar
150g plain flour

For the chocolate decoration. Put the chocolate in a heatproof bowl set over a saucepan of hot water and melt, stirring occasionally. Remove the bowl from the pan. Using a spoon, drizzle squiggly shapes of chocolate on to a silicone pastry mat or a tray lined with baking parchment. You will need four decorations, but it's a good idea to make extra in case you break any. Set aside in the fridge to set.

For the pannacotta. Combine the cream, milk, caster sugar, cocoa powder and vanilla seeds in a saucepan and heat until the mixture starts to come to the boil. Remove from the heat. Soak the gelatine in cold water for about 10 minutes to soften. Squeeze out the excess water and whisk into the cream mixture until melted. Set the pan in a bowl of iced water to cool it quickly.

Divide the mixture among four medium-sized dariole moulds. Place in the fridge and leave to set – this will take just over 2 hours.

For the caramelised pears. Peel and core the pears, then cut lengthways into equal wedges (you want 12). Spread the golden caster sugar on a plate and coat the pears with sugar. Put them in a hot frying pan to caramelise on all sides – this should take about 5 minutes. Carefully transfer to a plate and set aside until needed.

For the hazelnut biscuits. Preheat the oven to 160°C/Gas Mark 3. Spread the hazelnuts in a small baking tray and toast in the oven for 4-5 minutes or until golden. Tip into a food processor and blitz until finely ground.

Cream the butter and sugar together in a mixing bowl. Mix in the nuts and flour to make a biscuit dough. Roll it out on a lightly floured surface to 5mm thick. Using a 3cm round cutter, stamp out circles and arrange on a non-stick baking tray or a tray lined with baking parchment. Bake for about 25 minutes or until lightly coloured. The biscuits should be set on the base but soft on the top – they will harden as they cool. Transfer to a wire rack and leave to cool.

To serve. Dip each dariole mould in boiling water to release the pannacotta, then turn out on to a plate. Arrange three caramelised pear wedges on one side and three biscuits on the other. Place the chocolate decoration on top of the pannacotta.

ROSEMARY AND CHOCOLATE FONDANT
WITH AN ORANGE CHANTILLY CREAM MAKES 4

Chocolate is a wonderful thing, I'm sure most people would agree. You can infuse it with many flavours – even the weirdest things like mushrooms and tobacco work with it. Oranges are my favourite citrus fruit, and I like to use them to add sweetness to dishes as their flavour is quite mellow. Rosemary and orange is a perfect pairing that works really well with mackerel and lamb – and, I discovered, with chocolate too. Grandad gives this dessert the thumbs up and says it's 'top class'. I was going to cook it for the critics in the Semi-Finals, but because I made a chocolate fondant in the invention test for Marcus Wareing, this recipe wasn't used for the show.

125g unsalted butter, plus extra for
    greasing
1 tablespoon cocoa powder
1 sprig of rosemary
125g dark chocolate (at least 70% cocoa
    solids), broken up
2 eggs
2 egg yolks
125g caster sugar
2 tablespoons plain flour
icing sugar, for dusting
orange zest and rosemary leaves,
    to garnish

For the orange Chantilly cream
200ml double cream
1 tablespoon caster sugar
grated zest of 1/2 orange
1–2 tablespoons Cointreau

For the orange Chantilly cream. Put the cream and sugar in a mixing bowl and whip until thick. Add the orange zest and 1 tablespoon of Cointreau and whip the cream until it will hold semi-stiff peaks. Taste and add more Cointreau, if you like. Set aside in a cool place.

For the fondant. Preheat the oven to 180°C/Gas Mark 4. Grease four mini pudding moulds with butter, then dust the inside of each mould with cocoa powder – I put half the cocoa powder in one mould, then put two moulds together and shake. That way you can coat two at the same time, and they coat better.

Remove the leaves from the sprig of rosemary and put into a heatproof bowl with the chocolate and butter. Set the bowl over a pan of simmering water and melt gently, stirring. Remove from the pan and leave for about 5 minutes to cool slightly.

Whisk together the eggs, egg yolks and caster sugar in a large mixing bowl. Pass the chocolate mixture through a sieve into another bowl, to remove the rosemary, then mix into the egg and sugar mixture. Gently fold in the flour. Divide the chocolate mixture among the moulds and set them on a baking tray. Bake for about 12 minutes or until just set (you need to keep checking). Remove from the oven immediately and leave to rest for 30-60 seconds.

To serve. Turn out each fondant on to a serving plate (or serve the fondants in their moulds) and dust with a little icing sugar. Add a quenelle of orange Chantilly cream next to the fondant and scatter a little orange zest and rosemary on the plate.

Grandad gives this dessert the thumbs up and says it's top class.

A change to the classic tarte Tatin.

SPICED PLUM TARTE TATIN WITH THYME ICE CREAM SERVES 6

For our mass-catering challenge on *MasterChef*, cooking for the firemen, I suggested to Ollie and Louise that we do a spiced plum tart/cake. We ended up making a plum sponge, but the idea of spiced plum tart stuck in my head. So I thought, why not change a classic tarte Tatin to fit my flavour combo. Thyme complements plums well, so I decided to infuse the ice cream with thyme. I think it makes the perfect pairing.

For the ice cream
400ml double cream
200ml whole milk
a bunch of thyme sprigs (15g)
6 egg yolks
150g caster sugar

For the tarte Tatin
1 x 320g block of puff pastry, thawed if
    frozen
1 vanilla pod, split open
1 cinnamon stick
7 cloves
3 star anise
250g caster sugar
5 large, ripe but firm plums
25g unsalted butter
25g golden caster sugar

To finish
icing sugar, for dusting (optional)
a few picked thyme leaves

For the ice cream. Heat the cream with the milk in a heavy-based saucepan to 80°C. Remove from the heat and add the bunch of thyme. Leave to infuse for 45 minutes. Remove the thyme, then pass the creamy mix through a sieve into a clean pan. Heat again to 80°C.

Whisk together the egg yolks and caster sugar in a mixing bowl. When the creamy mixture has reached temperature, slowly whisk it into the egg yolk mix.
Pour back into the pan and gently cook, stirring with a wooden spoon, until the custard thickens enough to coat the back of the spoon. Pass the mixture through a sieve into a bowl. Leave to cool to room temperature.

Pour the custard base into your ice cream machine and churn according to the manufacturer's instructions. Transfer to a freezer container and keep in the freezer until ready to serve. (If made ahead and frozen hard, leave to soften at room temperature for 5 minutes before serving.)

For the tarte Tatin. Preheat the oven to 220°C/Gas Mark 7. For this recipe you need a 20cm tarte Tatin dish or ovenproof frying pan. Roll out the pastry on a floured work surface to a 26cm diameter round, or 3cm bigger than your dish or pan. Leave to rest until ready to assemble the tart.

Scrape the seeds from the vanilla pod and place in a saucepan with the pod, the cinnamon stick, cloves, star anise, caster sugar and 250ml water. Bring to the boil, stirring to dissolve the sugar, then boil for 2–3 minutes. Remove from the heat.

Cut the plums in half and remove the stones. Add the plums to the spiced syrup and poach for 3 minutes. Remove the plums with a slotted spoon and set aside. Reserve the syrup.

Heat the butter, golden caster sugar and 3 tablespoons of the spiced syrup in the tarte Tatin dish over a medium heat until golden brown and starting to form a caramel. Remove from the heat. Arrange the plums flesh side down in the dish.

Loosely roll up the pastry around the rolling pin, then carefully unroll over the top of the tart. Tuck the pastry down the sides around the fruit with your fingers. Bake for 30–35 minutes or until the pastry is crisp and golden. Remove from the oven and allow to settle for 10 minutes, then turn the tart on to a plate (set the inverted plate on top of the dish and, holding the two firmly together, quickly flip them over).

To serve. Cut the tart into wedges and place on the plates. Dust with icing sugar if you like. Add a good dollop of ice cream to each plate and scatter a few thyme leaves over the ice cream.

Larkin

I don't know why I love cooking so much. I could easily cook all day every day for the rest of my life. As a nipper, I used to watch cooking programmes back to back for hours on end. Despite this, owing to the commitment needed from my job as a solicitor, cooking took a place on the backburner and, strangely, before MasterChef I rarely cooked. However, that passion never died and I still day-dreamed, on a daily basis, about new dishes and concepts. I applied for MasterChef to see what I could achieve if pushed to the very limit. My Guinea Fowl and Lobster Smoked Paella with Citrus Air (page 139) is an example of that. I came up with the idea on the train back from the mass-catering challenge. I had a week to learn how to perfect a paella and to get the balance right between the smoke and the citrus. I would finish work and dash home to cook until the early hours and going into that showstopper round I still had a few tweaks to make. However, on the day I knew I had nailed it and I couldn't contain myself as a result. I improved so much during the competition but also learned that I still had a lot to learn. However, it has only made me want it more. I handed in my notice at work, and I am forging ahead to pursue a career in food I always dreamed of.

I was over the moon to be asked to write new recipes for this *MasterChef* cookbook. I think these dishes further reflect my personality and background: from The Triple Crown (page 106), which is a play on a 'rugby boy delicacy' and a nod to American fast food, to a Slow-cooked Beef Brisket (page 121) inspired by my childhood. For the Asian-themed dishes, it may take a trip to your local Chinese market or an online supplier, but it will be well worth it: the flavours are simply incomparable. Happy cooking!

PAN-FRIED HALIBUT, COCKLES AND PEANUTS

SERVES 4

This makes a great supper, which can easily be knocked up and on the table in 20 minutes. The cockles provide a rich depth to the sauce and go perfectly with the halibut. The peanuts add another dimension of flavour and a great contrast of texture.

4 pieces of halibut fillet (skin on), about 170g each
1 tablespoon rapeseed oil
salt and pepper to taste

For the coconut sauce
400ml canned coconut milk
1 tablespoon Thai red curry paste
1 Thai chilli, sliced
10 mangetouts, thinly sliced

For the cockles and peanuts
vegetable oil, for deep-frying
25g shelled peanuts
1 tablespoon vegetable oil
1 shallot, diced
100g shelled cockles
1 spring onion, thinly sliced
a pinch of caster sugar
1 tablespoon light soy sauce

For the coconut sauce. Whisk the coconut milk with the curry paste in a pan until smooth. Add the chilli and cook for about 2 minutes. Add the mangetouts and carry on cooking for 1 minute. Remove from the heat and set aside, ready to reheat for serving.

For the cockles and peanuts. Heat oil for deep-frying to 150°C, then fry the peanuts until golden. Scoop them out of the oil and drain on kitchen paper. Season and reserve.

Heat a wok with the 1 tablespoon oil. Add the shallot and fry for about 10 seconds to release the flavour (be careful not to burn it), then add the cockles, spring onion and sugar and stir-fry for a minute or so until hot, adding the soy sauce towards the end. Remove from the heat and keep hot.

For the halibut. Heat a non-stick frying pan over a moderate heat and add the rapeseed oil. Season the halibut fillets on both sides with salt and pepper, then lay the fish in the pan, skin side down. Gently fry until golden brown, then turn the fillets over and continue cooking for about 8 minutes.

To serve. Spoon the coconut sauce on to each plate. Arrange the cockles and peanuts around the plate and place the halibut on top.

A quick and easy supper.

DOVER SOLE, GINGER AND SPRING ONIONS

SERVES 4

This was inspired by one of my mum's recipes. The freshness of the ginger and spring onions with the delicate Dover sole, and the rich flavour of the shaoxing rice wine makes a really delicious dish. All I added to Mum's recipe was the fish-bone cracker and a sauce thickened by modern methods. As you can imagine, it took a lot of trial and error to get the cracker right, but when you do – wow!

4 Dover sole
vegetable oil, for deep-frying
200g cornflour

For the stock
200ml chicken stock
2g cellulose gum (see method)
0.5g xanthan gum (see method)

For the vegetables
1–2 tablespoons vegetable oil
a bunch of Chinese celery, trimmed and
    sticks cut into 5cm julienne
1 onion, cut into 5cm julienne
1 carrot, cut into 5cm julienne
3 spring onions, 2 cut into 5cm julienne
    and 1 thinly sliced
60g fresh ginger, peeled and cut into
    5cm julienne
3 tablespoons shaoxing rice wine
1 teaspoon caster sugar
2 tablespoons light soy sauce
1 teaspoon toasted sesame oil
1 tablespoon cornflour, mixed with
    3 tablespoons water
salt and pepper to taste

For the Dover sole. Skin each fish, then remove the fillets, keeping the 'carcass' whole. Keep the four carcasses to make the fish-bone crackers. Slice the sole fillets into thumb-sized pieces, following the grain of the fish; set aside.

For the stock. Mix together the chicken stock, cellulose gum and xanthan gum in a saucepan over low heat, stirring until thickened. (If you don't use the cellulose gum and xanthan gum, you can thicken the vegetable mixture by adding more cornflour; see below.) Season to taste, then set aside.

For the fish-bone crackers. Heat oil for deep-frying to 170°C. Make the fish-bone crackers one at a time. Spread the cornflour on a tray and dredge the carcass, patting off any excess cornflour. Holding the tail, lower the fish carcass head first into the hot oil so the carcass curls. (Press a wok ladle against the middle of the carcass to help it curl as you are lowering it into the oil – this will start to set the shape of the fish-bone cracker.) When the tail almost reaches the oil let go of it so it slides into the oil. Keep the ladle on the centre of the carcass while you fry it for 2–3 minutes or until it is golden brown and crisp. Carefully remove the cracker and drain on kitchen paper. Keep the crackers hot.

To cook the fish. Lower the temperature of the deep-frying oil to 150°C. Drop the pieces of fish into the hot oil and flash-fry for about 5 seconds or until the fish is just cooked. Remove and drain on kitchen paper.

For the vegetables. Set a wok on high heat and add the vegetable oil. When it is hot, add all the julienne vegetables and the ginger and stir-fry for about 10 seconds. Add the rice wine and shake the wok to help evaporate the alcohol, then add the hot thickened chicken stock. Add the pieces of fish and the sugar and toss in the wok to mix with the vegetables (the sugar will balance the acidity of the rice wine and bring out the flavour of the fish). Add the light soy sauce and sesame oil and toss everything in the wok to mix together. Stir in enough of the cornflour mixture to thicken (start with 1 teaspoon if you have used the gums to thicken the stock, or 1 tablespoon without the gums; if it is all looking a bit thin, add more of the cornflour mix). Check the seasoning.

To serve. Place a curled fish bone cracker on each plate. Spoon the fish and vegetables into the cracker with enough sauce to coat them. Garnish with the sliced spring onion.

One of my favourite dishes from the show.

PAN-FRIED SEA TROUT WITH POMEGRANATE
AND FENNEL SALAD AND A TERIYAKI DRESSING   SERVES 4

Easy and light with really fresh flavours. Perfect for a summer lunch.

4 pieces of sea trout fillet (skin on),
    about 175g each
25g unsalted butter
juice of 1/2 lemon
1 tablespoon finely shredded pickled
    ginger

For the teriyaki dressing
200ml light soy sauce
50g caster sugar
1 gelatine leaf

**For the pomegranate
and fennel salad**
1 bulb of fennel, with fronds
1 pomegranate
100g podded and skinned baby broad
    beans (fresh or frozen)
1 teaspoon olive oil
salt and pepper to taste

For the teriyaki dressing. Put the light soy sauce in a saucepan with the sugar and bring to the boil. Lower the heat and simmer for 15 minutes. Remove from the heat. Soak the gelatine in cold water for about 2 minutes to soften, then squeeze out excess water and add to the soy sauce. Stir until the gelatine has melted, then leave to cool and thicken.

For the salad. Trim the top and bottom off the fennel, reserving the fronds. Thinly slice the fennel bulb lengthways (use a mandolin if you are brave enough). Cut the pomegranate in half and take out the seeds. Combine the fennel, pomegranate seeds and broad beans in a bowl and add the olive oil. Gently fold together. Season to taste.

For the sea trout. Score the skin of the fish. Heat the butter in a non-stick frying pan. When it starts to sizzle, carefully lay the fish in the pan, skin side down, and gently fry for about 8 minutes or until the skin is crisp and golden and most of the flesh has changed colour with just the top still raw.

Carefully turn the fillets over and squeeze the juice from the lemon half over them. Cook for a further 1 minute, basting the fish with the lemony pan juices. Remove from the heat.

To serve. Smear the teriyaki dressing across each plate. Set a trout fillet in the centre and arrange the fennel salad alongside. Garnish with pickled ginger and the fennel fronds.

LARKIN CEN

91

PAN-FRIED WILD SEA BASS, PORK BELLY
AND SHIITAKE MUSHROOM WONTONS

SERVES 4

Sea bass needs salt, so I flavoured the filling for the wontons here with pancetta and soy, and I used a strong Thai ingredient – lemongrass – to give the dish a distinctive aroma. It was a lot of work getting the balance right in this dish so I hope you like it. I remember on the day I cooked it that John Torode came over to my workstation and said *gai choi* was his favourite vegetable of all time. I have to agree with him!

1 bunch of *gai choi* (Chinese mustard greens), about 500g
1–2 tablespoons rapeseed oil
4 large fillets of sea bass (preferably wild sea bass)
shredded spring onions, to garnish

For the lemongrass consommé
100g dried shiitake mushrooms
5 stalks of lemongrass, outer leaves removed, roughly chopped
2 garlic cloves, crushed
50g fresh ginger, peeled, sliced and crushed
25g sugar

For the enoki mushrooms
50g enoki mushrooms
1 large spring onion

For the wontons
300g skinless pork belly, diced
50g pancetta, diced
a handful of fresh shiitake mushrooms, cut into small cubes
1 tablespoon caster sugar
1 teaspoon cornflour
1 teaspoon salt
1 spring onion, finely chopped
2 teaspoons light soy sauce
2 teaspoons toasted sesame oil
16 wonton wrappers
oil for deep-frying
salt and pepper to taste

For the lemongrass consommé. Put the dried shiitake mushrooms in a saucepan with 1.2 litres water. Bring to the boil, then gently simmer for 5 minutes to release the mushrooms' flavour. Add the lemongrass, garlic, ginger and sugar and stir to mix. Simmer gently for a further 15 minutes. Remove from the heat and leave to infuse for 15 minutes. Strain the consommé through a muslin-lined sieve into a clean saucepan. Season to taste. Set aside, ready to reheat for serving.

For the enoki mushrooms. Wash thoroughly under cold running water, then cut off the base of the mushroom clusters. Divide into four bunches. Tie each bunch together with a leaf from the spring onion. Set aside.

For the wontons. Combine the pork belly, pancetta and shiitake mushrooms in a mixing bowl. Stir together the sugar, cornflour, salt, spring onion, light soy sauce and sesame oil in another bowl, then mix into the pork mixture. Work the mixture to break it up and tenderise it by lifting it all up out of the bowl in a handful and then throwing it back into the bowl as hard as you can. Do this for about 2 minutes.

To make each wonton, put a bit of the pork mixture in the centre of a wonton wrapper and bring all the corners together over the filling to form a parcel. Squeeze the corners together to seal. If made ahead, cover with clingfilm and refrigerate. Before serving, heat oil for deep-frying

to 150°C. Drop half of the wontons into a saucepan of boiling water on a medium heat and simmer for about 5 minutes until cooked through (break one in half to test). Remove with a slotted spoon and drain on kitchen paper; keep hot. Put the remaining wontons into the hot oil and deep-fry for about 3 minutes or until golden brown and crisp. Remove and drain on kitchen paper; keep hot.

For the *gai choi*. Halve the *gai choi*, then cut into finger-size pieces. Cook the *gai choi* in a saucepan of boiling water for about 4 minutes or until tender. Drain and keep warm.

For the sea bass. Heat a large frying pan over a medium heat, then add the oil. Place the fillets in the pan, skin side down, and cook for about 2 minutes or until crisp. Turn the fish over and remove the pan from the heat. Leave the fish to cook in the residual heat of the pan for 1 minute.

To serve. For each serving, place a large metal chef's/presentation ring (bigger than the sea bass fillet) in a soup plate. Arrange *gai choi* around the inside of the chef's ring, to line it, then put boiled wontons in the centre. Remove the ring. Place shredded spring onions, a bundle of enoki mushrooms and fried wontons on top. Set a sea bass fillet against this. Ladle hot consommé into the soup plate.

Making Pan-fried Wild Sea Bass, Pork Belly and Shiitake Mushroom Wontons (see page 92).

MASTERCHEF | THE FINALISTS COOKBOOK

LARKIN CEN

ASIAN 'SMOKY' CONFIT SALMON WITH CAVIAR

SERVES 4

This dish shows off the benefits of cooking sous-vide: perfectly cooked, melt-in-the-mouth confit salmon. Soy sauce is one of those fascinating ingredients that brings out the flavour in savoury dishes, and coupled with the taste of the sea from the caviar and the crunchiness of the black fungus makes for a really classy starter.

10g dried black fungus (wood ear or
    cloud ear)
1 x 1kg skinned centre-cut salmon fillet,
    pin-boned

For the scented oil
300ml grapeseed oil
50g piece of fresh ginger, peeled and cut
    in half
2 large bunches of spring onions, roughly
    chopped
4 garlic cloves, crushed
50g coriander seeds
a strip of lemon peel
2 sprigs of lemon thyme
a bunch of coriander, roughly chopped

For the soy dressing
150ml light soy sauce
1 tablespoon mirin
40g caster sugar
salt and pepper to taste

To garnish
4 tablespoons caviar
coriander shoots
cherrywood smoking chips for the
    smoking gun

For the scented oil. Heat the grapeseed oil in a saucepan to 40°C. Add the ginger, spring onions, garlic, coriander seeds, lemon peel, lemon thyme and chopped coriander. Maintain the heat of the oil at 40°C for 15 minutes, then remove from the heat and leave to infuse for 10 minutes. Pass the oil through a fine sieve into a jug. Set aside.

For the black fungus. Put the dried black fungus in a bowl, pour over 200ml boiling water and leave to soak for 30 minutes. Drain and cut into julienne. Return to the empty bowl and dress with 1 teaspoon of the scented oil. Season and reserve.

For the salmon. Slice the salmon fillet across into eight strips. Place in a vacuum bag with 6 tablespoons of the scented oil. Seal and compress, then cook in a water bath at 42°C for 25 minutes. Lift out of the water bath and reserve in the bag. (If you don't have a vacuum-pack machine and a water bath, heat all the scented oil in a pan on a low heat until it is lukewarm, about 60°C, add the salmon and cook for 7 minutes to set the protein.)

For the soy dressing. Heat the soy sauce, mirin and sugar together in a small saucepan, stirring until the sugar has dissolved. Set aside.

To serve. Place a piece of salmon on each plate and place another piece diagonally across the top. Add the dressed black fungus to one side of the salmon and a quenelle of caviar to the other. Finish the salmon with some drops of scented oil and season, then garnish with coriander shoots. Set a small glass dome on top to cover the salmon, caviar and black fungus. Using a smoking gun, fill the glass chamber with smoke by lifting one side of the glass dome and putting the tube of the gun into the gap. Once the glass dome is full of smoke put it back down to seal in the smoke. Serve the soy dressing in little jugs.

MACKEREL WITH SMOKED EEL
AND CUCUMBER MOUSSE AND BLACK BEAN PURÉE SERVES 4

Mackerel has had a bit of a revival lately. Here I've put my own Asian-inflected spin on this very versatile fish, which I've balanced with a light eel and cucumber mousse.

4 mackerel fillets (skin on)
freshly cracked pepper and coarse sea salt
2 tablespoons sunflower oil
coriander cress, to garnish

For the mirin vinaigrette
25ml soy sauce
25ml mirin
1 garlic clove, peeled
125ml rapeseed oil

For the black bean purée
2 garlic cloves, peeled
2 Thai chillies, diced
100g preserved black beans
50g caster sugar
2 tablespoons dark soy sauce

For the smoked eel and cucumber mousse
4 tablespoons crème fraîche
1 tablespoon milk
2 teaspoons snipped chives
2 teaspoons grated fresh horseradish
2 tablespoons crisp-fried shallots, drained
100g cucumber, peeled, deseeded and diced
salt and pepper to taste
120g smoked eel

For the mirin vinaigrette. Combine the soy sauce, mirin and garlic clove in a medium saucepan and heat gently. Remove from the heat and set aside to infuse for 2 hours. Discard the garlic, then pour into a bowl. Add the rapeseed oil and whisk vigorously to emulsify. Set aside.

For the black bean purée. Drop the garlic cloves into a blender and blend briefly. Add the chillies and carry on blending to a purée. Scrape into a large saucepan and add the preserved black beans, sugar and soy sauce. Mix well. Add 100ml water and blend together using a hand blender. Bring to the boil, then turn the heat down and simmer for about 20 minutes or until thick. If you like, pass the mixture through a fine sieve so that it is very smooth. Set aside.

For the smoked eel mousse. Mix together the crème fraîche and milk in a bowl. Fold in the chives, horseradish, fried shallots, cucumber and seasoning to taste. Remove the skin and any bones from the eel and flake the flesh. Fold into the crème fraîche mixture. Keep in the fridge until needed.

For the mackerel. Remove any pin bones from the mackerel, then rinse the fish under cold running water. Dry thoroughly on kitchen paper and lightly season with sea salt and cracked pepper. Heat a non-stick frying pan with the sunflower oil. Place the mackerel fillets skin side down in the hot oil and fry gently until the skin becomes crisp. Turn the fillets over and finish cooking – about 3 minutes longer. Drain on kitchen paper.

Lay the mackerel fillets on a plate and cut each one in half, then baste with the mirin vinaigrette. Leave to infuse while dressing the plate.

To serve. Make a swipe of black bean purée on each plate. Shape the mousse into a quenelle and place on the plate. Add the mackerel fillets. Garnish with coriander cress, or other mixed cresses, and drizzle vinaigrette round the plate.

Mackerel is such a versatile fish.

GRILLED AUBERGINE WITH ONION BHAJIS AND BOMBAY ALOO SERVES 4

Who said vegetarian food couldn't be exciting? I would happily destroy every bit of this plate! The three different components come together to make this a very special spicy dish.

2 aubergines
2 tablespoons olive oil

For the Bombay aloo base
1 tablespoon curry powder
1 tablespoon ground cumin
1 tablespoon paprika
1½ tablespoons ground turmeric
1 tablespoon ground coriander
1½ teaspoons garam masala
2 carrots, chopped
2 onions, chopped
1 x 400g can chopped tomatoes

For the Bombay aloo
1 tablespoon vegetable oil
1 onion, sliced
2 teaspoons garlic and ginger paste
2 teaspoons curry powder
2 teaspoons chilli powder
2 tablespoons tomato purée
400g new potatoes, boiled and cut in half
chopped coriander, to garnish

For the onion bhajis
1 red onion, finely sliced
1 garlic clove, finely chopped
1 teaspoon finely chopped fresh ginger
1½ teaspoons melted butter
1 teaspoon chilli powder
¼ teaspoon ground turmeric
3 tablespoons gram flour
1½ tablespoons rice flour
¼ teaspoon fennel seeds
a handful of coriander leaves, chopped
oil for deep-frying
salt to taste

For the Bombay aloo base. Put all the ingredients, except the canned tomatoes, into a large saucepan and add enough water just to cover the vegetables. Cover and cook on a very low heat for 2 hours. Add the tomatoes, then pour into a blender and blend to a purée. Set aside.

For the Bombay aloo. Heat the oil in another pan and fry the onion with the garlic and ginger paste for 1 minute or until slightly browned. Add the curry powder, chilli powder and tomato purée and cook for 2–3 minutes, stirring. Add the Bombay aloo base and bring to the boil. Once bubbling add the potatoes. Set aside, ready to reheat when needed.

For the grilled aubergines. Preheat the grill to medium and heat a ridged griddle pan until very hot. Cut the aubergines lengthways into eight 1cm slices. Brush the cut surfaces with olive oil. Place on the griddle pan (in batches, if necessary) and rotate the slices to give them nice charred marks on both sides. As they are chargrilled, transfer the aubergine slices to a baking tray. Place under the grill and grill for about 15 minutes or until soft, turning the slices over halfway through the time. Roll up each slice tightly, then cover and keep warm in a low oven until ready to serve.

For the onion bhajis. Mix together the sliced onion, garlic, ginger and melted butter. Add the chilli powder, turmeric, gram flour, rice flour, fennel seeds, chopped coriander and salt to taste. Sprinkle with 2 tablespoons water and mix well – the mixture should be thick enough to hold its shape (add a little more water if the mixture seems too dry).

Heat oil for deep-frying to 170°C. With moistened hands, take tablespoon-sized portions of the onion mixture and drop gently into the hot oil, then fry for about 5 minutes or until golden brown on both sides and cooked through (this will make about eight bhajis). Drain the fried bhajis on kitchen paper.

To serve. Heat the Bombay aloo, then spoon on to serving plates. Top with the aubergine rolls and hot onion bhajis. Garnish with coriander.

ASIAN MIXED STARTERS

SERVES 4

FROM THE SERIES

When I cooked this on MasterChef, the elements of the dish were arranged in a particular way. Every component was placed just so, sometimes balancing precariously. Feel free to be creative, presenting the starters in your own way.

For the prawn spring rolls and tofu sheet rolls
200g peeled raw king prawns
10g cornflour
1 teaspoon toasted sesame oil
1 egg
4 sheets spring roll pastry
4 dried tofu sheets

For the vegetable spring rolls
1 carrot, cut into julienne
1 onion, cut into julienne
50g drained canned sweetcorn, chopped
4 sheets spring roll pastry

For the tofu emulsion
5 pieces of preserved/fermented tofu,
    about 50g in total
1 garlic clove, crushed
1 teaspoon sugar

For the soy-poached chicken and soy reduction
300ml light soy sauce
100ml dark soy sauce
3 star anise
50g sugar
2 skinless boneless chicken breasts
1 tablespoon cornflour

For the steamed egg with crab
2 eggs
100ml chicken stock
a dash of toasted sesame oil
1 spring onion, thinly sliced
100g fresh white crab meat

For the stir-fried cockles
40g shelled unsalted peanuts
1 tablespoon vegetable oil
150g shelled cockles
4 teaspoons light soy sauce
4 spring onions, finely sliced

For the morning glory
a splash of olive oil
1 garlic clove, chopped
1 tablespoon preserved/fermented tofu
a bunch of Chinese morning glory
salt and pepper to taste

oil for deep-frying
violas or other edible flowers, to garnish

For the prawn spring rolls. Toss the prawns with the cornflour and sesame oil in a bowl. Break the egg into another bowl. Take a pinch of the egg white and add to the prawns, then whisk the remaining egg with a fork just to mix. Tip the prawns on to a board and dice using a Chinese cleaver. Use about half of the prawn mix for the spring rolls and the remainder for the tofu sheet rolls.

For each spring roll, lay a sheet of spring roll pastry on the work surface and put about a tablespoon of the prawn filling into the centre, making a cigar shape. Take the bottom corner of the pastry sheet and fold to the centre over the filling. Bring the two side corners towards the centre. The pastry should now look like an open envelope with the filling inside. Roll the envelope over towards the top corner and seal with

beaten egg. Keep, covered, in a cool place until ready to fry.

For the tofu sheet rolls. Make the tofu sheet rolls in the same way as the prawn spring rolls, using the remainder of the prawn filling and beaten egg for sealing. Cover and set aside in a cool place.

For the vegetable spring rolls. Mix together the carrot, onion and sweetcorn in a bowl. Use to fill the spring roll pastry sheets, then fold, roll and seal with beaten egg in the same way as the prawn spring rolls. Cover and set aside in a cool place.

For the tofu emulsion. Put the preserved tofu and garlic in a small saucepan and cook over a medium heat for about 5 minutes. Transfer to a blender and blend with the sugar until smooth (or blend in the pan with a hand blender). Return the mixture to the pan and cook on a low heat, stirring, to make a smooth paste. Set aside until needed.

For the soy-poached chicken. Put the soy sauces, star anise and sugar in a saucepan. Taste and add more sugar if needed – there should be enough to balance the acidic taste of the uncooked soy sauce. Bring to the boil. Place the chicken breasts in the liquid and bring back to the boil, then remove from the heat. Cover the pan and leave the chicken in the poaching liquid for 30 minutes or until cooked through.

continued on page 104

continued from page 103

Remove the breasts (reserve the poaching liquid for the soy reduction) and cut each into four equal pieces. Keep warm.

For the soy reduction. Pour 100ml of the chicken poaching liquid into a small pan, bring to the boil and reduce by half. Mix the cornflour with 1 tablespoon water to form a paste, then whisk into the reduction to thicken. Set aside.

For the steamed egg with crab. Prepare a large steamer that will hold four small (50ml) ramekins. Put the eggs in a bowl, add a pinch of salt and the chicken stock and whisk well together. Add the sesame oil and spring onion to the egg mixture, then fold in the crab meat. Fill the ramekins with the mixture. Set them in the steamer and steam on a low heat for 8–10 minutes or until set. Keep warm.

To finish the spring rolls and tofu sheet rolls. Heat oil for deep-frying to 150°C. Deep-fry the prawn spring rolls for 3–4 minutes or until golden brown all over and crisp. Remove and drain on kitchen paper, then keep hot. Deep-fry the tofu sheet rolls and then the vegetable spring rolls in the same way; drain and keep hot.

For the stir-fried cockles. Deep-fry the peanuts in the hot oil until golden brown. Remove with a slotted spoon and drain on kitchen paper. Heat the vegetable oil in a frying pan, add the cockles and flash-fry to reheat. Add the peanuts, soy sauce and spring onions and stir-fry briefly. Remove from the heat and keep hot.

For the morning glory. Heat the oil with the garlic in a wok on a low heat for about 10 seconds. Add the preserved tofu and cook for 1 minute. Add the morning glory, season and stir-fry until wilted.

To serve. Arrange some forks and spoons (ideally including Chinese spoons) on each plate or piece of slate. Use as many items of cutlery as you like. Place the starters on or attached to the cutlery or placed randomly on the plate. Pour the soy reduction and the tofu emulsion into sauce dipping bowls or saucers and set them on the plate. Place the steamed egg with crab in its ramekin on the plate. Garnish the plate with edible flowers.

Describe your first food memory...

Making ramen. I was only a nipper and I wanted to make a noodle-in-broth dish like my mum made them. All I could find in the fridge was some pak choi, an egg and some frankfurters. I used them all... the result was delicious!

Thoughts on your co-finalists?

I have a lot of respect for Dale and Nat and we have become good friends. I have always said MasterChef is like an extreme team building exercise. I like the way we got to the Final from our own individual strengths which made for a great final episode.

THE TRIPLE CROWN

SERVES 4

For the slider buns
25g custard powder
270ml milk
1 teaspoon caster sugar
15g unsalted butter
375g white bread flour
1/2 x 7g sachet fast-action dried yeast
1 teaspoon salt
beaten egg or milk, for glazing
sesame seeds, for sprinkling

For the Thousand Island dressing
50g mayonnaise
1 tablespoon tomato ketchup
1 1/2 teaspoons white wine vinegar
1 teaspoon caster sugar
1 teaspoon sweet chilli sauce
1/2 teaspoon finely chopped white onion

For the Southern-fried chicken
1 teaspoon crushed black peppercorns
1/2 teaspoon each of paprika and
    onion powder
1/4 teaspoon each of dried sage, dried
    thyme and ground allspice
1 teaspoon salt
100g plain flour
1 egg
100ml milk
4 chicken drumsticks
vegetable oil, for deep-frying

For the burgers
2 teaspoons vegetable oil
1 shallot, finely chopped
800g minced fillet steak
olive oil, for brushing
4 rashers of smoked streaky bacon
a handful of mixed salad leaves
8 slivers of pecorino cheese
salt and pepper to taste

To garnish
3 gherkins, diced
Maldon salt (optional)

For the slider buns. Whisk the custard powder with the milk in a saucepan, then place over the heat and cook, stirring often, until boiling. Stir in the sugar and butter. Pour into a mixing bowl and leave to cool until lukewarm.

Add the flour, yeast and salt and mix to a firm dough. Cover and leave for 10 minutes. Knead the dough lightly on a floured work surface until smooth, then return the dough to the bowl, cover again and leave to rise in a warm place for about 1 1/2 hours or until doubled in size.

Knock back the dough to deflate it, then divide equally into eight portions (50g each). Shape each piece into a ball. Place them, well spaced apart, on a large baking tray lined with baking parchment. Cover and leave to rise in a warm place for about 1 hour or until doubled in size.

Preheat the oven to 200°C/Gas Mark 6. Brush the tops of the buns with egg wash or milk and scatter over some sesame seeds. Bake for about 12 minutes or until the buns are golden brown and sound hollow when tapped on the base. Cool on a wire rack. Split the buns open for serving.

For the dressing. Combine all of the ingredients in a small bowl, seasoning with a pinch each of salt and pepper, and stir well. Set aside.

For the Southern-fried chicken. Put the crushed peppercorns, paprika, onion powder, herbs, allspice and salt in a mortar and grind to a powder with the pestle. Mix with the flour in a mixing bowl. Lightly beat the egg with the milk in another mixing bowl.

Turn the chicken into lollipops: using a knife, cut around the bone at the less meaty end of each drumstick, freeing the meat and tendons. Grasp the bottom of the drumstick with one hand and with the other push the meat to the top: the meat will remain attached to the bone and form a ball. Clean the exposed bone with a dry cloth, removing any fat and cartilage.

Before serving, heat oil for deep-frying to 180°C. Dip the chicken in the egg mixture, then coat with the flour mixture. Deep-fry for about 12 minutes or until golden and cooked through. Drain on kitchen paper. Keep hot.

For the burgers. Heat the oil in a small pan and fry the shallot until soft; leave to cool. Mix the shallot with the minced steak and season. Divide into eight portions and shape each into a 1cm-thick burger. Heat a frying pan. Brush both sides of the burgers with olive oil, then fry for about 20 seconds on each side or until well browned (they will be rare in the middle – cook for longer if you like, to taste). Remove from the pan and keep hot.

Fry the bacon in the pan, then cut into eight rectangles the same size as the burgers.

To serve. Assemble half of the sliders by spooning some Thousand Island dressing into each of four buns, then add a burger, some mixed leaves and a slice of pecorino. Make the other sliders with dressing, a burger, a slice of pecorino and two pieces of bacon. Slice a small bit off the bottom of each drumstick so that it can stand upright on the plates. Add the sliders and garnish with gherkin cubes. If you like, finish the plates with a sprinkle of Maldon salt and freshly ground black pepper.

It's a rugby boy thing: if you can eat a KFC, a Burger King and a McDonald's in one sitting you win the coveted 'triple crown'! Here is a more manageable version, and slightly more refined, I hope!

SINGAPORE CHICKEN AND UDON NOODLE HOT WOK   SERVES 4

The thick udon noodles work perfectly in this dish. They are sold vacuum-packed in supermarkets so you can keep them in your storecupboard.

2 tablespoons vegetable oil
4 chicken thighs (skin on)
4 chicken drumsticks (skin on)
1 garlic clove, crushed
1 bird's eye chilli, diced
2 tablespoons Madras curry paste
200ml chicken stock or water
1 tablespoon cornflour
3 tablespoons frozen peas
1 red pepper, deseeded and cut into julienne
1 green pepper, deseeded and cut into julienne
1 red onion, halved and thinly sliced lengthways
16 raw tiger prawns, peeled and butterflied
400g fresh udon noodles
4 tablespoons chopped coriander

Heat a wok, then add the vegetable oil. Put the chicken thighs and drumsticks in the wok and cook over high heat for about 5 minutes or until browned all over; the skin should become golden and crisp.

Lower the heat a bit and allow the oil to cool down slightly, then add the garlic and chilli to flavour the oil. Add the curry paste and stir around the wok, making sure all the chicken pieces are coated with the mixture. Pour in the stock or water. Lower the heat to medium and simmer for 30 minutes or until the chicken is cooked through (check by cutting into a thigh or drumstick to the bone and having a look at the flesh inside).

About 5 minutes before the end of the cooking time, stir the cornflour with 3 tablespoons water in a small bowl. Stir again before adding to the wok. Mix into the sauce and carry on cooking to thicken.

Add the peas, peppers, red onion, prawns and udon noodles to the wok. Stir-fry for 5 minutes, mixing the ingredients into the sauce.

To serve. Divide among four bowls and garnish with coriander.

A fantastic all-in-one dish.

BEEF TEPPANYAKI WITH CONFIT SHALLOT AND SHALLOT PURÉE

SERVES 4

I love the richness of shallots with steak. This is a really classy dish, fit to grace any dinner party.

For the shallot purée
85g unsalted butter
800g shallots, roughly chopped
1 bay leaf
150ml double cream

For the confit shallots
500g goose fat or olive oil
4 banana shallots, peeled
3 garlic cloves (unpeeled)
3 sprigs of thyme

For the teppanyaki
4 fillet steaks, about 110g each
vegetable oil, for frying
1½ tablespoons honey
1½ tablespoons light soy sauce
salt and pepper to taste
thyme leaves, to garnish

For the shallot purée. Melt the butter in a large pan over a medium heat and stir in the shallots and bay leaf. Season with salt, then lower the heat, cover and leave to sweat very gently for 40–50 minutes or until soft and translucent. Pour in the double cream, stir and boil for 1 minute.

Remove from the heat. Put the shallots in a blender (remove the bay leaf) and blend until smooth, adding just enough of the cooking liquid to allow them to purée – you want to have a thickish consistency. Push through a sieve into a small saucepan and set aside, ready to reheat for serving.

For the confit shallots. Heat the fat or oil in a saucepan over a low heat. Add the shallots, garlic and thyme and cook gently for 45 minutes – the fat should be bubbling very, very slowly. Use a slotted spoon to remove the shallots from the fat; discard the garlic and thyme.

Just before serving, heat a small frying pan, add the shallots and sear until golden brown on all sides. Remove from the pan and keep warm.

For the teppanyaki. Trim each fillet steak into a neat rectangular shape. Heat up a heavy-based frying pan and add a splash of vegetable oil. Place the steaks in the pan and sear for 20 seconds on each side to brown. Try to keep the shape of the steak by compressing the sides with tongs.

Remove the steaks from the pan. Mix the honey and soy together well and then, using a pastry brush, brush the mixture on to both sides of the steaks and season with salt and pepper. Leave the beef to rest for 10 minutes.

To serve. Place a steak on each plate with the confit shallots and spoonfuls of shallot purée. Drizzle the steak juices from the frying pan round the plate, then garnish with thyme and a sprinkling of freshly ground black pepper.

Simple, yet so elegant.

FILLET STEAK IN BLACK BEAN SAUCE, PAK CHOI, WITH ASPARAGUS FRIED RICE SERVES 4

My weakness has got to be perfectly cooked steak. So it was only fitting that I cooked steak at least once on the show.

1 red pepper
500g piece of fillet steak
olive oil, for frying
2 knobs of butter
2 medium heads pak choi, each cut in half
    lengthways
micro cress, to garnish
salt and pepper to taste

For the fried rice
400g jasmine rice, rinsed
2 tablespoons vegetable oil
150g asparagus, woody ends removed
    and sliced at an angle
2 eggs, beaten
1 onion, finely chopped
2 tablespoons light soy sauce
1 teaspoon toasted sesame oil
a bunch of spring onions, finely sliced

For the black bean sauce
a handful of dried shiitake mushrooms
200g preserved black beans
4 Thai chillies, finely sliced
4 garlic cloves, finely chopped
100g caster sugar
20ml dark soy sauce

For the roasted pepper. Roast the red pepper over a gas flame on the hob or under a preheated hot grill until the skin is charred all over. Place the pepper in a bowl, cover with clingfilm and leave to cool for 20 minutes. Peel the blackened skin off the pepper, then cut it in half and remove the seeds. Slice into 2.5cm-wide strips. Set aside until needed.

For the fried rice. Put the rice in a rice cooker and add enough water to come 8mm above the surface of the rice. Steam the rice for 10–12 minutes, or according to the rice cooker's instructions, until the rice is tender. If you don't have a rice cooker you can use a large saucepan. Transfer the rice to a bowl, cover and cool. (While the rice is cooking and cooling, you can prepare the remaining elements of the dish.)

Just before serving, heat the oil in a wok over high heat until smoking hot, then add the asparagus, eggs and onion and quickly stir-fry until hot and the eggs are softly cooked. Add the rice and toss until the grains are separated and the rice is piping hot. Add the soy sauce, sesame oil and spring onions and toss in the wok to mix.

For the black bean sauce. Soak the shiitakes in 300ml boiling water for 10 minutes. Strain the soaking water; discard the shiitakes. Mix together the preserved black beans, chillies, garlic, sugar and soy sauce in a large saucepan. Add 200ml of the shiitake soaking water and bring to the boil, then reduce the

heat and simmer for 15–20 minutes or until the sauce is thick. Set aside, ready to reheat for serving.

For the steak. Preheat the oven to 110°C/Gas Mark 1/2. Heat a large ovenproof frying pan on a high heat, add some oil and sear the steak on all sides to brown. Remove from the heat. Add the butter to the pan and baste the steaks with the foaming melted butter, then place the pan in the oven and roast for 30 minutes, for medium rare. Remove and leave to rest for at least 10 minutes before serving.

For the pak choi. Blanch the pak choi in a large pan of boiling water for 2 minutes. Drain and refresh in iced water. Just before serving, heat a wok with a little oil over a high heat, add the pak choi and stir-fry quickly until lightly golden. Season.

To serve. Spoon black bean sauce on each plate. Slice the fillet steak into four and place one piece on top of the black bean sauce on each plate. Arrange the pak choi next to the steak, and the pepper strips on top of the steak. Serve the asparagus fried rice in a small bowl on the plate. Garnish the plate with some micro cress.

A great comfort food dish.

CHILLI BEEF AND PINEAPPLE FRIED RICE

SERVES 4

Fried rice is one of my number one comfort foods. You can go red or green with the chilli, depending on how hot you like your dish.

4 sirloin steaks, about 250g each
vegetable oil, for cooking
salt and pepper to taste
1 red chilli (or green, if you prefer it less spicy), thinly sliced, to garnish
a handful of chopped coriander, to garnish

For the pineapple fried rice
230g long-grain rice
1 tablespoon vegetable oil
1 red onion, diced
1 egg
flesh from 1 pineapple, cut into cubes
1 tablespoon curry powder
1 bird's eye chilli, diced
1 tablespoon light soy sauce
1 tablespoon chilli oil, or to taste

For the rice. Rinse the rice until the water is clear. Put the rice into a saucepan (or use a rice cooker) and add enough water to come about 1.5cm above the surface of the rice. Bring to the boil, then lower the heat to a simmer, cover with a lid and cook for 15–20 minutes or until the rice is tender and all the water has been absorbed. When ready, fluff up the rice using a fork and set aside.

For the steaks. Heat a ridged griddle pan. Brush the steaks with a little vegetable oil and season on both sides with salt and pepper, then place the steaks on the hot pan. After a few minutes, turn the steaks 90 degrees, to give them diamond-patterned grill marks.

Turn the steaks over and repeat on the other side, then continue chargrilling until cooked to your liking: for rare steaks, after browning them on both sides as described, cook for an additional 30 seconds on each side; for medium rare, cook for an additional 1–1^1/$_2$ minutes on each side; cook for an additional 2–2^1/$_2$ minutes on each side for well done (exact cooking times will depend on the thickness of the steaks). Remove the steaks from the pan and leave to rest.

To finish the rice. While the steaks are resting, heat a wok over a high heat. Add the vegetable oil and then the onion and flash-fry for 5 seconds. Add the egg and scramble in the pan with a cooking spoon. Add the pineapple, curry powder and chilli and stir-fry for about 30 seconds.

Add the rice to the wok and stir into the pineapple mixture using a wooden spoon until the grains are separate. Season with the light soy sauce and 1 teaspoon salt (or to taste). Finally, add the chilli oil (add more if you like it a bit hotter).

To serve. Spoon the rice into bowls, add the sliced steak and garnish with the sliced chilli and chopped coriander.

FILLET STEAK TARTARE AND SEARED SCALLOP
WITH HOISIN SAUCE AND ASIAN PEAR SERVES 4

FROM THE SERIES

The concept of 'surf and turf' has evolved over the years from the original steak and lobster. For my take, with steak tartare and scallops, it was really challenging getting the balance of the dish right. Along with my wonton dish it got me through to the Quarter-Finals, so it's a dish I am proud of.

For the steak tartare
250g beef fillet, well trimmed
1 tablespoon very finely diced *zha cai* (preserved mustard root)
1 teaspoon each of Tabasco sauce, Dijon mustard, toasted sesame oil, rapeseed oil and acacia honey

For the hoisin sauce
3 tablespoons hoisin sauce
1 tablespoon each of crushed yellow bean sauce, shaoxing rice wine, caster sugar
1 tablespoon light soy sauce, or to taste
1 tablespoon dark soy sauce, or to taste

For the seared scallops
olive oil, for frying
4 hand-dived scallops, shelled
juice of 1 lemon
salt to taste

To garnish
1 Asian pear
a good pinch of caster sugar
4 quail's eggs
100g shelled edamame beans
violas, chive blossoms or other edible flowers
micro coriander
toasted sesame oil, for drizzling

For the steak tartare. Dice the steak into very small cubes. Combine the remaining ingredients in a bowl and mix well together. Season with salt. Add the beef and toss to coat, then set aside in a cool place until needed.

For the Asian pear. Peel and core the Asian pear, then cut into fine dice. Put into a small bowl of water, add a good pinch of sugar and set aside.

For the hoisin sauce. Put the hoisin sauce and crushed yellow bean sauce into a saucepan and stir in the rice wine and sugar. Add 250ml water and simmer on a medium heat, stirring occasionally, for about 10 minutes or until the sauce is the consistency of thick honey. Add the light and dark soy sauces to taste. Set aside.

For the seared scallops. Heat a heavy frying pan with a good layer of olive oil until smoking hot. Add the scallops to the pan and sear for 1–2 minutes or until golden brown on one side. Turn over and sear on the other side. Remove from the pan and season with a squeeze of lemon juice and salt to taste. Keep hot.

To serve. For each serving, set a metal chef's/presentation ring on the plate and spoon in the steak tartare; lift off the ring. Carefully crack open a quail's egg. Separate the white and yolk; discard the white and place the yolk back into a shell half. Set this on top of the steak tartare. Place a scallop next to the tartare. Arrange pear dice on the plate around the tartare and scallop. Make two 'swooshes' of hoisin sauce on either side of the arranged tartare and scallop. Scatter the edamame, violas and micro coriander on the plate. Swirl some sesame oil around to finish.

Surf 'n' turf!

Making Fillet Steak Tartare and Seared Scallop with Hoisin Sauce and Asian Pear (see page 116).

LARKIN CEN

Simple, tender and delicious.

SLOW-COOKED BEEF BRISKET WITH BRAISED MOOLI

SERVES 4

I love this dish. Beef brisket is one of my favourite cuts of meat – cook it very slowly on the lowest heat possible to ensure tenderness. The bitterness from the mooli works perfectly with the brisket. Serve with noodles or some steamed rice.

2 tablespoons vegetable oil
3 garlic cloves, peeled
1 x 400g piece of beef brisket
150ml hoisin sauce
3 tablespoons light soy sauce
6 star anise
100g caster sugar
700g mooli
4 spring onions, roughly chopped
salt and pepper to taste
a handful of chopped coriander, to garnish

Heat the oil in a large saucepan, add the garlic cloves and leave to infuse on a low heat for about 1 minute. Scoop out the garlic and reserve. Increase the heat, add the beef brisket and fry until lightly golden all over.

Add the hoisin sauce, soy sauce, star anise, 450ml water and the sugar to the saucepan and bring to the boil. Turn down the heat to a simmer.

Peel the mooli, then chop into uniform chunks (around 5 x 2.5cm). Add the mooli, spring onions and reserved garlic to the pan and stir well. Cover the pan with the lid slightly ajar, to allow some steam to escape, and simmer for 2 hours. Taste and season as needed.

To serve. Remove the brisket and cut into four pieces. Spoon the braised mooli into four serving bowls, top with the brisket and garnish with coriander.

CHAR SUI WITH KIMCHI

SERVES 4

Char sui – pork belly marinated in a savoury hoisin-based sauce and then roasted – is melt-in-the-mouth-addictive. Pungent kimchi provides a great accompaniment. Feel free to buy the kimchi if you don't want to wait the weeks for it to ferment.

For the kimchi
75g caster sugar
20g salt
1 Chinese cabbage
100g garlic cloves, peeled
65ml fish sauce
65ml light soy sauce
50g chilli powder
40g roughly chopped spring onions
30g roughly chopped carrot
7g dried shrimps (optional)

For the char sui
450ml hoisin sauce
50g caster sugar
5 tablespoons dark soy sauce
150g crushed yellow bean sauce
2 garlic cloves, peeled
1 x 800g pork belly
2 tablespoons maltose
shiso leaves, to garnish

For the kimchi. Combine 30g of the sugar with the salt in a bowl. Rub this mixture into all the leaves of the Chinese cabbage. Put it in the bowl, cover with clingfilm and leave in the fridge for 12 hours.

Drain off the liquid from the cabbage and discard. Put the rest of the ingredients and the remaining sugar in a blender and blend into a rough purée. Rub this mixture into the cabbage leaves in the bowl. Cover and leave to ferment at 18–24°C for 2–4 weeks (the longer you leave it, the more intense the flavour). Before serving, cut the vegetable apart roughly.

For the char sui. Mix together the hoisin sauce, sugar, dark soy and crushed yellow bean sauces, garlic and 300ml water in a blender. Blend to a purée. Pour this marinade into a mixing bowl.

Cut the skin from the pork belly and discard. (You can cook the skin separately as crackling if you wish, and use to garnish the final dish, though I prefer to serve it without.) Cut the pork belly vertically into two even, long pieces. Place the pork in the marinade and turn to coat all over, then cover and leave to marinate in the fridge for at least 1 1/2 hours.

Preheat the oven to 200°C/Gas Mark 6. Remove the pork from the marinade and place it in a roasting tray. Roast for 30 minutes. In the meantime, pour the marinade into a small saucepan, add a splash of water and bring to the boil. Simmer for 30 minutes. Set this sauce aside.

Make a maltose solution by mixing the maltose with 2 tablespoons water in a bowl. When you take the pork out of the oven, use a pastry brush to cover the pork with the maltose solution. Cut the pork into slivers.

To serve. Serve the char sui with shiso leaves, the kimchi and the hoisin sauce.

Melt-in-the-mouth-addictive.

ROAST AND BRAISED SUCKLING PIG,
WITH FONDANT POTATO, CELERIAC PURÉE, CAVOLO NERO
IN A CIDER ORANGE JUS SERVES 4

FROM THE SERIES

Couldn't go to Italy and not cook suckling pig! So many wonderful flavours come together in this dish, but it's all about the different cuts of meat and their different preparations.

1 whole suckling pig, jointed (saddle, shoulder and 2 hind legs)

For the roast saddle
1 bulb of garlic, cut across in half
3 tablespoons balsamic vinegar
4 onions, cut into wedges
1 bunch of celery, roughly chopped
leaves from a bunch of sage

For the rolled leg
cloves from 2 bulbs of garlic, crushed
1 tablespoon balsamic vinegar

For the braised shoulder
olive oil
330ml medium cider
2 garlic cloves, crushed
200ml chicken stock
50g sugar
a bunch of parsley, finely chopped

For the cider orange jus
100g caster sugar
330ml medium cider
500ml orange juice
10 cloves
5 star anise
3 cinnamon sticks
10 cardamom pods

For the fondant potatoes
4 large Maris Piper or Desiree potatoes
2 tablespoons vegetable oil
a knob of butter
2 sprigs of thyme
300ml chicken stock

For the celeriac purée
1 whole celeriac, about 400g, peeled and diced
75g unsalted butter
500ml double cream

For the cavolo nero
1 large head of cavolo nero, tough stalks removed, shredded
20g unsalted butter
juice of 1/2 lemon
salt and pepper to taste

For the suckling pig. Trim the saddle, keeping the meat on the bone. Remove the bone from each leg using a boning knife and the back of a chef's knife. Remove the skin from the shoulder and take all the meat off the bone. Cut the meat into 2.5cm pieces.

For the roast saddle. Preheat the oven to 200°C/Gas Mark 6. Rub the cut side of one half of the garlic bulb all over the saddle. Rub the balsamic vinegar onto the skin followed by some salt. Stuff the cavity of the saddle with the onions, celery, sage and the remaining garlic half. Put the saddle in a large roasting tin and roast for 20 minutes.

For the rolled leg. Meanwhile, lay out the two boned legs on a tray, skin side down. Season the flesh side with salt and pepper and place the garlic on top. Roll up each leg and tie into shape with string. Rub the balsamic vinegar over the skin and season with salt.

Once the saddle has had its initial 20 minutes of roasting, place the rolled legs in the roasting tin with the saddle. Continue roasting for 25 minutes, then reduce the oven temperature to 160°C/Gas Mark 3 and roast for a further 15 minutes or until both the saddle and legs are cooked through. Once cooking has finished, leave the saddle and legs to rest for about 15 minutes before carving to serve. (While the saddle and legs are roasting, you can prepare the remaining elements of the dish.)

For the braised shoulder. Add some olive oil to a medium frying pan over a high heat and sear the pieces of shoulder until browned all over. Add the cider and garlic to the pan along with the chicken stock and sugar. Bring to the boil, then reduce the heat to medium and cook for 5–10 minutes or until the liquid is syrupy. Season with salt and pepper and mix in the parsley. Remove from the heat and set aside, ready to reheat for serving.

For the cider orange jus. Melt the sugar in a frying pan, then cook for 5 minutes or until a caramel forms. Add the cider and orange juice and mix well with the caramel. Add the cloves, star anise, cinnamon and cardamom and leave to infuse on a very low heat for 30 minutes. The jus should be syrupy, thick enough to coat the back of a spoon. Pass through a sieve into a clean pan and set aside, ready for reheating.

continued on page 126

continued from page 125

For the fondant potatoes. Peel the potatoes and cut out a cylinder from each one using a 5cm metal cutter. Neaten the top and bottom of the cylinders with a knife so they are flat. Run the knife around the sharp edges to smooth them.

Heat the oil in a sauté pan and place the potatoes in the pan flat side down. Fry until golden brown. Turn the potatoes over onto the other flat side and fry until golden. Add the butter and thyme, then pour in enough chicken stock to come halfway up the potatoes. Lower the heat to medium-low, cover and cook for about 25 minutes or until tender.

For the celeriac purée. Put the celeriac, butter and cream in a saucepan and gently simmer on a medium heat for about 25 minutes or until tender. Drain the celeriac, reserving the cooking liquor, and tip into a food processor. Blitz until smooth, adding some of the cooking liquor to achieve a smooth purée. Season. Keep warm or transfer to a pan for reheating.

For the cavolo nero. Put the cavolo nero into a saucepan with the butter and 2–3 tablespoons water. Cook on a medium heat for about 5 minutes or until wilted. Remove from the pan and season with the lemon juice, salt and pepper. Keep hot.

To serve. Carve the saddle and legs. Arrange the saddle, legs and shoulder in the centre of each plate. Make two teardrops of celeriac purée on the plate. Set a fondant potato and a pile of cavolo nero next to the suckling pig. Drizzle round the cider orange jus.

MasterChef highlights and lowlights?

Cooking my braised pork belly dish. It reminded me of my late grandad and my mum. It was a classic Chinese dish which I took apart and put back together.

My soufflé fiascos. When picking up my soufflé from the floor I briefly considered serving it up and calling it a 'de-constructed' chocolate soufflé!

Three last things to eat before you die...

Pak choi.
Sirloin steak.
Pork belly.

My favourite of all the dishes I cooked on MasterChef; this is a classic southern Chinese dish that I took apart and put back together. Cooked perfectly, the skin of the pork belly will melt in your mouth. I had to use a pressure cooker due to time constrictions, but it's better to slow-cook the pork if you can.

BRAISED PORK BELLY IN ROSE WINE
WITH CHRYSANTHEMUM, TARO, LOTUS ROOT CRISPS AND A FENNEL KIMCHI

SERVES 4

For the rose wine sauce
150ml hoisin sauce
100ml Chinese rose wine (*mei kuei lu chiew*)
4 garlic cloves, peeled
2cm piece of fresh ginger, peeled
50g caster sugar
3 tablespoons Chinese five-spice powder
3 tablespoons dark soy sauce
50g crushed yellow bean sauce
6 star anise

For the braised pork belly and taro
1 x 500g piece pork belly (preferably Spanish Ibérico), skin on
2 litres chicken stock
2 bay leaves
1 tablespoon vegetable oil
1 small taro, about 300g

For the fennel kimchi
1 bulb of fennel
2 tablespoons yellow bean and chilli paste
1 tablespoon grapeseed oil
1 tablespoon fish sauce
1 teaspoon sugar

For the lotus root crisps
1 fresh lotus root
1 teaspoon sugar
oil for deep-frying

For the chrysanthemum greens
1 head of *tong ho choi* (chrysanthemum greens)
salt and pepper to taste

edible violas, to garnish

For the rose wine sauce. Put the hoisin sauce, rose wine, garlic, ginger, sugar, five spice, soy sauce and yellow bean sauce in a blender and blend until smooth. Transfer to a large bowl and add the star anise and 600ml water. Stir to mix. The consistency should be like a béchamel sauce, so add more water if needed. Set aside.

For the pork belly and taro. Heat a frying pan (without oil) until smoking hot. Place the pork belly skin side down in the pan and sear until the skin is toasted. Remove from the heat. Scrub off any burnt bits from the pork skin under cold running water.

Put the chicken stock and bay leaves in a deep frying pan and bring to the boil. Lower the heat, then place the pork in the pan and poach for about 10 minutes. Remove the pork and dry with a kitchen cloth; discard the stock and bay leaves. Heat the oil in the pan, then return the pork, skin side down, and fry over a medium heat for about 5 minutes to render the fat. Take the pork out of the pan and add to the rose wine sauce.

Peel the taro and cut into 2.5–3cm cubes. Add to the rose wine sauce. Pour the mixture into a flameproof casserole; if necessary, add some water so the pork is almost covered with liquid. Cover and cook over a medium heat for about 2 hours or until the pork is very tender; check halfway through the cooking and add more water if the mixture is too dry. Alternatively, you can braise in a pressure cooker for 40–50 minutes. (While the pork is being braised, make the kimchi and prepare the lotus root and chrysanthemum greens.)

Remove the pork belly and taro. Cut the belly into four equal pieces. Keep the pork and taro warm. Pass the sauce through a fine sieve into a saucepan. Check the seasoning – if the sauce tastes too strong or is too thick, add a touch of hot water. The sauce should have a nice glossy finish. Set aside, ready to reheat for serving.

For the fennel kimchi. Trim the fennel bulb (reserve the fronds for garnish), then thinly slice it lengthways. Combine the bean and chilli paste, oil, fish sauce and sugar in a blender and blend together. Add to the fennel and mix so all the slices are coated. Put the fennel mixture in a vacuum bag, seal and compress. (If you don't have a vacuum-pack machine you can use a plastic food bag, with the air pressed out before sealing.) Leave to infuse for at least 2 hours.

For the lotus root crisps. Using a Japanese mandolin, slice the lotus root into very thin discs. Put them into a container with the sugar and water to cover; set aside. Just before serving, drain the slices and pat dry with kitchen paper, then deep-fry in oil heated to 150°C until crisp and golden. Drain and season with salt. Keep hot.

For the chrysanthemum greens. Roughly cut up the greens, then blanch in a pan of boiling water until wilted. Drain well and season. Keep hot.

To serve. Set a piece of pork belly in the centre of each plate and add some taro. Drizzle with the rose wine sauce. Put some fennel kimchi on the plate and scatter the chrysanthemum greens and lotus root crisps around – the presentation should look as natural as possible. Garnish with some violas and fennel fronds.

HAM HOCK CONGEE WITH SARDINES AND CHINESE CRULLERS SERVES 4

Congee isn't really mainstream here, but it is a very popular dish in southern China.
I hear that Australians love it too, so I wonder if John is a fan?

For the congee
1 x 1.3kg unsmoked ham hock
150g long-grain rice
2.5cm piece fresh ginger, peeled and cut into 'coins'
salt and pepper to taste

For the Chinese crullers
1 teaspoon dried yeast
1 teaspoon caster sugar
2 tablespoons plus 250ml lukewarm water
1 teaspoon bicarbonate of soda
1 teaspoon baking powder
300g white bread flour
1 teaspoon salt
vegetable oil, for deep-frying

For the sardines
8 sardines, heads removed and cleaned
50g seasoned flour
1 tablespoon light soy sauce
juice of 1 lime

To garnish
2.5cm piece fresh ginger, peeled and cut into julienne strips
3–4 spring onions, thinly sliced

For the ham hock. Put the ham hock in a large saucepan, cover with cold water and bring to the boil. Reduce the heat and blanch for 1 minute. Drain off the water and refresh the hock under cold running water for a minute or so. Drain off this water, then pour in enough fresh cold water to cover and bring to a simmer. Cover the pan and leave to simmer gently 2 hours.

Lift out the hock. When it is cool enough to handle, pull the meat from the bone and tear it apart; set aside until needed. Reserve 500ml of the poaching liquid.

For the congee. Pour the reserved poaching liquid into a large pot, add 700ml fresh water and the rice, and bring to the boil. Add the ginger coins. Turn the heat down to low, cover with the lid slightly ajar (to allow steam to escape) and cook, stirring occasionally, for 1–1¼ hours or until the rice mixture is thick and creamy. Set the congee aside, ready to reheat for serving.

For the Chinese crullers. Mix the yeast and sugar with the 2 tablespoons lukewarm water and leave for 10–15 minutes to get foamy.

Pour the 250ml lukewarm water into another bowl and mix in the bicarbonate of soda and baking powder. Sift the flour and salt into a large mixing bowl. Add the yeast and the soda mixtures to the flour and mix together with a wooden spoon to make a dough. Knead on a floured work surface for about 5 minutes or until smooth and elastic (if the dough seems too sticky at first, work in a little bit more flour). Return to the bowl, cover with clingfilm and leave to rise in a warm place for about 2 hours or until doubled in size.

Turn out the dough on to the well-floured surface. Sprinkle some flour on the dough, then roll out into a long rectangle. Cut across into 16 strips 2.5cm wide. Pair up the strips, placing one on top of the other. Leave to rest for 5 minutes. In the meantime, heat oil for deep-frying to 150°C.

Lay a chopstick across the top of one of the doubled strips, in the middle, and press down to seal the two strips together. Repeat the process with the remaining doubled strips. Fry the crullers in batches so you don't crowd the pan: hold each end of a doubled strip and pull gently to stretch the dough a little, then lower into the hot oil. Deep-fry, turning constantly, for 2–3 minutes or until puffy and golden brown. Drain on kitchen paper and keep hot. Turn up the heat under the pan of oil so the temperature rises to 170°C.

For the sardines. Score the skin of the sardines. Dredge the fish with seasoned flour, then lower into the hot oil and deep-fry for about 2 minutes or until crisp. Drain on kitchen paper.

To serve. Put a ladleful or two of congee into each serving bowl. Add some ham hock and garnish with ginger and spring onions. Serve with the hot Chinese crullers and the sardines seasoned with the soy sauce and lime juice.

THE CHINESE THREE ROAST DINNER

SERVES 4

This one was for my family and my grandad – I always said if I got to the Final I would cook this dish. The key to the crispiest crackling is bone-dry pork skin that has been treated with vinegar and salt, and the key to crisp duck skin is a really fatty duck and to separate the fat from the meat. Get your bike pump and hairdryer out, folks...

For the Cantonese roast pork
1 tablespoon bicarbonate of soda
1 x 1kg piece pork belly with a good layer of fat (skin on)
2 tablespoons malt vinegar
450ml hoisin sauce
150g crushed yellow bean sauce

For the Cantonese roast duck
1 medium duck
200ml Chinese vinegar
3 tablespoons maltose
2 tablespoons Chinese five-spice powder
5 star anise
cherrywood chips for oven smoker (optional)

For the char sui
450ml hoisin sauce
75g sugar
50ml dark soy sauce
150g crushed yellow bean sauce
2 garlic cloves, finely chopped
1 x 200g piece pork belly, skin removed
2 tablespoons maltose

For the *choi sum*
a bunch of *choi sum* (Chinese flowering cabbage)
a splash of olive oil

For the plum noodles
6 plums, pitted and roughly chopped
75g sugar
1 glass red wine
1.6g agar agar

For the glutinous rice parcel
a handful of dried shiitake mushrooms
400g glutinous rice, well rinsed
20g pancetta, finely diced

20g *lap chung* (Chinese sausage), finely diced
1 teaspoon cornflour
2 teaspoons light soy sauce
1 garlic clove, finely chopped
1 spring onion, finely sliced
4 dried lotus leaves, soaked in warm water to rehydrate
salt and pepper to taste

To garnish
1 cucumber
edible roses

For the Cantonese roast pork. Fill a large pan with water and bring to the boil. Add the bicarbonate of soda, then put the pork belly into the water. Boil for 1 minute. Lift out of the water and drain on a tray (discard the water). Score the skin, then rub in the vinegar and season with salt.

Mix the hoisin sauce with the crushed yellow bean sauce in a bowl and season. Make slashes about 2.5cm deep in the flesh side of the pork belly. Rub the hoisin mixture over the flesh, making sure the mixture gets into the slashes.

Using a hairdryer, blow-dry the pork belly all over for 10 minutes, being careful not to cook it. Hang the pork up using a meat hook, hanging it near a floor fan (and over newspaper). Let the fan carry on blow-drying the meat for about an hour or until it is bone dry. Alternatively, instead of hanging up the pork you can just leave it, skin side up, to dry at room temperature for a day.

When you are ready to start roasting the pork, preheat the oven to 275°C/the highest gas mark. Line a curved roasting rack with baking parchment (to help prevent the hoisin mixture from falling off the pork while it is roasting) and set the rack over a roasting tray. Put the pork on the rack and roast for 40 minutes. Reduce the oven temperature to 200°C/Gas Mark 6 and roast for a further 20 minutes or until the pork is cooked through. If the skin is not crisp enough, roast for an extra 5–10 minutes.

Remove from the oven and leave to rest for at least 30 minutes before cutting into rectangular or square portions for serving.

For the Cantonese roast duck. Make an incision in the duck's neck, then separate the skin from the flesh in that incision. Insert the tube of a bicycle pump into the neck incision and pump in air so that the skin becomes separated from the flesh. The duck will inflate like a balloon.

Next, hang the duck on a meat hook with newspapers underneath, or put it in a roasting tin. In a wok, heat the Chinese vinegar with the maltose. Set the wok under the duck on the newspaper, or next to the roasting tin. Baste the skin of the duck with the vinegar mixture, using a wok ladle, for 1 minute. Transfer the duck to a draining rack. Discard the vinegar mixture.

There is an opening at the tail end of the duck where you can get into the cavity

continued on page 134

continued from page 133

between the skin and flesh. Fill the cavity with the five spice, star anise and some salt. Use a small metal skewer to close the skin at the opening. Hang the duck up on a meat hook like the pork belly and blow-dry in front of the floor fan for 1 hour.

When you are ready to roast the duck, preheat a second oven to 200°C/ Gas Mark 6. If using, place an oven smoker in the oven with the cherrywood chips (these will give the duck a slightly smoky taste). Place the duck on a rack in a roasting tin and roast for 30 minutes. Reduce the oven temperature to 140°C/ Gas Mark 1 and roast for another 30 minutes. Leave to rest for 30 minutes before removing the duck breasts and slicing them for serving.

For the char sui. Mix together the hoisin sauce, sugar, dark soy sauce, crushed yellow bean sauce, garlic and 300ml water in a large bowl. Place the pork in this marinade and turn to coat. Cover and leave to marinate in a cool place for at least an hour (or preferably overnight).

When ready to cook, remove the pork from the marinade (reserve this) and place in a roasting tray. Put into the first oven (at 200°C/Gas Mark 6) with the Cantonese roast pork. Roast for 30 minutes. Remove and set aside to rest for 30 minutes.

Meanwhile, put the marinade into a small saucepan with a splash of water and bring to the boil, then boil for 10 minutes. Set aside, ready to reheat for serving. Mix the maltose with 250ml warm water in a small bowl.

Before serving, use a pastry brush to cover the pork with the maltose mixture, then thinly slice.

For the *choi sum*. Cut the *choi sum* into pieces about 10cm long. Blanch in a pan of boiling salted water for 3 minutes. Drain and refresh in iced water, then set aside. Just before serving, add a splash of oil to a wok on a high heat and stir-fry the *choi sum* for 30 seconds.

For the plum noodles. Combine the plums, sugar and red wine in a saucepan and cook for 10 minutes or until soft. Pass through a sieve and then through muslin into a measuring jug to get a plum liquor. If necessary make up to 100ml with water.

Pour into the clean saucepan and mix in the agar agar. Bring to the boil, then remove from the heat. Fill a medium syringe with the warm plum gel. Pump the gel into a syringe tube that is about 20cm long. Immediately place the syringe tube in a bowl of ice and leave to cool and set.

Before serving, use an empty syringe of the same size to pump air into one end of the tube. This will push the plum noodles out of the other end of the tube.

For the glutinous rice parcel. Soak the dried shiitakes in a bowl of boiling water for about 10 minutes or until they are soft. Drain the shiitakes and cut into julienne; set aside. Put the rice in a rice cooker and pour in enough water to come about 8mm above the surface of the rice, then cover and steam the rice for 10–12 minutes, or according to the rice cooker's instructions, until the rice is tender. If you don't have a rice cooker you can use a large saucepan.

Meanwhile, stir-fry the pancetta and *lap chung* in a wok for about 2 minutes, then add the shiitakes. Mix the cornflour with 1 tablespoon water to make a paste. Add to the wok and mix with the pancetta and *lap chung*. Add the soy sauce and season, then stir in the garlic and spring onion. Set this filling aside.

For each parcel, take a handful of the glutinous rice and place in the middle of a soaked lotus leaf. Using the palm of your hand press the rice down so that it is flat. Add a quarter of the filling to the middle of the flattened rice. Take the bottom corner of the lotus leaf and pull it up over the rice – the rice should follow the lotus leaf and roll over so the filling is enclosed. Hold down that corner with your thumb and bring the side corners in so that the shape now resembles an open envelope. 'Seal' the envelope by bringing in the final top corner of the lotus leaf and pressing lightly.

Before serving, put the parcels into a steamer and steam for about 10 minutes. Keep hot.

For the cucumber. Using a vegetable peeler, take four lengthways strips from the cucumber (don't use the first strip you take, which will be mainly skin – you want the four strips to have skin just at the sides). Reserve for the garnish.

To serve. Arrange the pork, duck and char sui diagonally across the middle of each plate. Drizzle over the hoisin sauce marinade from the char sui. Put the *choi sum* next to the meat. Roll a cucumber strip into a cylinder and place in front of the meat. Set a glutinous rice parcel on the plate behind the meat. Add the plum noodles to the plate. Scatter rose petals randomly on the plate.

Food Heaven & Hell?

Food heaven would be a
Sunday roast dinner with
roast pork and crackling and
all the trimmings, of course!

Food hell would be a salad.
I don't mind them as an
accompaniment to a main
course, but otherwise no!

VENISON SASHIMI WITH TOBACCO-INFUSED PEKING SAUCE AND WASABI MAYONNAISE

SERVES 4

The smoky flavour of the tobacco-infused sauce gives a unique dimension to this plate. It's probably the most unusual Peking sauce you will ever taste, and my own creation.

1 x 400g venison fillet
salt to taste

For the tobacco-infused Peking sauce
100g caster sugar
2.5g rolling tobacco
4 tablespoons hoisin sauce
1 tablespoon crushed yellow bean sauce
1 tablespoon shaoxing rice wine

For the wasabi mayonnaise
1½ teaspoons wasabi powder
1 egg yolk
1½ teaspoons white wine vinegar
150ml sunflower oil

To garnish
1 bulb of fennel
Chinese celery leaves (or normal celery leaves)
1 tablespoon shredded pickled ginger

For the tobacco-infused Peking sauce. Put the sugar and 2 tablespoons water in a medium saucepan and cook to a light caramel. Add the tobacco and leave on a very low heat to infuse for 30 minutes. Remove from the heat and cool for about 5 minutes, then strain into a bowl and stir in the rest of the sauce ingredients. Set aside.

For the wasabi mayonnaise. Mix the wasabi with 4 teaspoons water in a bowl to form a paste. Mix in the egg yolk and vinegar, then gradually whisk in the oil to make a thick, creamy mayonnaise. Keep in the fridge until needed.

For the venison. Trim the venison into a neat rectangular shape and wrap tightly in clingfilm. Place in the freezer to firm up for 1½ hours before slicing the venison into paper-thin slices using a mandolin. (If you do not want to use a mandolin, you can use a knife but only freeze the venison for 30 minutes.) Put the slices in a bowl and leave to come to room temperature. Season with a pinch of salt.

For the fennel. Slice the fennel lengthways into thin slivers using a mandolin or sharp knife.

To serve. Arrange the venison on the plates. Add dots of mayonnaise and drizzles of Peking sauce, then garnish with Chinese celery leaves, fennel and pickled ginger.

Wonderfully comforting flavours and textures.

GUINEA FOWL AND LOBSTER SMOKED PAELLA WITH CITRUS AIR   SERVES 4

I came up with this dish on the train, on the way back from the mass-catering round. Up until that point I had never cooked a paella. But I drew up a concept, researched it and then spent hours making paella after paella after paella. My first few attempts tasted horrendous, but in the end the result was amazing. Unfortunately my waistline took a hammering! Gregg described this dish as 'beautifully flavoured food', which will do for me.

For the guinea fowl
2 boneless guinea fowl crowns
  (2 breasts on each crown)
3 knobs of unsalted butter
1 tablespoon plain yoghurt
2 sprigs of lemon thyme
2 garlic cloves, crushed
olive oil, for frying

For the smoked paella
1 x 400g can tomatoes
2 garlic cloves, peeled
1 onion, quartered
cherrywood smoking chips for the
  smoking gun
16 fresh clams, cleaned
8 fresh mussels, scrubbed and debearded
1 large glass medium white wine
2 pinches of saffron threads
20g Ibérico chorizo, cut into 5mm cubes
20g pancetta, cut into 5mm cubes
1 tablespoon olive oil
100g paella rice (Bomba or Calasparra)
1 tablespoon smoked paprika
500ml chicken stock
100g peas (shelled fresh or frozen)
2 tablespoons chopped parsley
juice of 1/2 lemon

For the citrus air
100ml fresh orange juice
100ml fresh lime juice
80ml fresh lemon juice
80g caster sugar
a pinch of salt
2g de-oiled soya lecithin
0.5g xanthum gum

For the lobster tail
oil for deep-frying
200g cornflour
2 raw lobster tails, shell removed and
  each cut in half lengthways
30g smoked paprika

For the black pudding
40g good-quality black pudding, cut into 4
  slices
1 tablespoon vegetable oil
salt and pepper to taste

To garnish
red amaranth
lemon essence

For the sous-vide guinea fowl. Season the guinea fowl crowns and put into a vacuum bag with two knobs of butter, the yoghurt, lemon thyme and garlic. Seal and compress, then cook in a water bath at 60°C for 1 hour. (If you don't have a vacuum-pack machine and a water bath, you can use a deep saucepan, a digital thermometer and some clingfilm, although the resulting texture won't be exactly the same. Heat water in the pan to 60°C. Meanwhile, wrap the guinea fowl and flavourings tightly in three layers of clingfilm. Pierce the clingfilm with a skewer to release any air, then wrap up with a final, very tight layer to seal. Place in the pan of water and cook for 1 hour, keeping the temperature constant by raising or lowering the heat, or moving the pan on and off the flame.) Remove from the water bath

and set aside, in the bag, until needed. (While the guinea fowl is being cooked, make the other elements of the dish.)

Before serving, remove the guinea fowl crowns from the bag and sear on the skin side in a hot pan with a knob of butter and a bit of oil until golden brown. Cut each crown in half to separate the breasts.

For the smoked paella. Put the canned tomatoes, garlic and onion in a food processor and blitz until smooth. Using a smoking gun, fill the processor bowl with smoke through the feed tube. Pulse-blitz the tomato mixture for about 2 minutes while the smoke is going in to make sure it gets incorporated. Set aside, covered, to let the smoke be fully absorbed into the tomato mixture.

Put the clams and mussels in a hot pan, add the white wine and cover with the lid. Steam for 5 minutes to open the shells. Using a slotted spoon, remove the clams and mussels from the pan. When they are cool enough to handle, take them from their shells and set aside. Strain the cooking juices and reserve.

Add the saffron to 250ml of hot water and leave to infuse. Meanwhile, fry the pancetta and chorizo with the olive oil in a paella pan. Add the smoked tomato sofrito and cook for 3–4 minutes.

continued on page 140

continued from page 139

Next add the paella rice and stir into the sauce. Add the paprika, saffron water and enough of the chicken stock just to cover the rice. Stir in 2 tablespoons of the reserved clam and mussel juices. Bring just to a simmer, then lower the heat and cook for about 25 minutes or until the rice is al dente, adding more stock when needed. About 5 minutes before the end of the cooking, fold in the peas and parsley. (Prepare the lobster, citrus air and black pudding while the paella is cooking.)

Before serving, raise the heat under the pan so that the bottom of the paella gets slightly crisp. Add the lemon juice, clams and mussels, and check the seasoning.

For the citrus air. Mix together all the ingredients in a large glass bowl or measuring jug. Use a foaming wand to create a thick layer of bubbles on the surface. Leave to settle for about 10 minutes.

For the lobster tail. Heat oil for deep-frying to 150°C. Spread the cornflour on a tray and dredge the lobster tails all over, shaking off excess cornflour. Deep-fry for 3–4 minutes or until cooked. Remove and drain on kitchen paper, then dust with smoked paprika and season with salt. Keep hot.

For the black pudding. Cut each slice of black pudding into a triangle. Pan-fry in a hot pan with the oil for about 30 seconds or until slightly caramelised on both sides. Keep hot.

To serve. Spoon the paella into the centre of each soup plate. Arrange a lobster tail half, seared guinea fowl breast and triangle of black pudding on the paella and put some red amaranth on top. Spoon some citrus air on to the rice. Cover the plate with a glass cloche and fill the inside with smoke using the smoking gun. Dab a cloth with lemon essence and swipe around the edges of the plate, to clean it and give a lemony aroma.

DUCK CURRY SERVED WITH CANDIED ORANGE PILAU RICE AND THICK-CUT CHIPS SERVES 4

FROM THE SERIES

This is a Welsh delicacy – curry 'alf and 'alf (half rice and half chips). I discovered you can't get it in England, so here is my tribute to that great Welsh institution, with triple-cooked chips and a candied orange pilau rice.

4 Aylesbury duck breasts
coriander shoots, to garnish

For the curry sauce
5 Thai chillies
20g garlic cloves, peeled
20g fresh ginger, peeled
100g cashew nuts
2 Thai shallots, peeled
a handful of coriander, roughly chopped
1 teaspoon paprika
1 teaspoon smoked paprika
2 tablespoons garam masala
1 tablespoon ground turmeric
1 tablespoon vegetable oil
70g butter
100g pure creamed coconut
300ml chicken stock
1 tablespoon tomato ketchup
1 teaspoon tomato purée
3 tablespoons sugar
100ml plain yoghurt

For the pilau rice
400g basmati rice
25g caster sugar
100ml orange juice
finely pared peel of 1 orange, cut into
    julienne
1 teaspoon saffron threads
75g unsalted butter
1 tablespoon sunflower oil
a 2.5cm piece of cinnamon stick
8 green cardamom pods, crushed
1 tablespoon ground turmeric
1 teaspoon cumin seeds
2 small shallots, finely sliced
1 dried bay leaf

For the chips
4 large Maris Piper potatoes
oil for deep-frying
sea salt
salt to taste

For the curry sauce. Combine the chillies, garlic, ginger, nuts, shallots, chopped coriander and spices with a touch of water in a blender or spice mill and blend together to make a paste. If the paste is too thick, add a splash more water. Set aside.

Heat up a large saucepan with the oil on a medium heat. Add the butter and creamed coconut and heat until melted. Add the curry paste and stir well. Add the stock, ketchup, tomato purée and sugar. Bring just to the boil, then simmer gently, stirring occasionally, for about 40 minutes or until you have a thick sauce-like consistency. Season to taste, then set aside. (While the sauce is simmering, prepare the rice and chips.)

Before serving, add the yoghurt to the curry sauce and stir until incorporated, then reheat gently. Pass the curry sauce through a sieve into a jug.

For the pilau rice. Rinse the rice in a sieve to remove the excess starch, until the water runs clear. Tip the rice into a bowl, cover with fresh water and set aside to soak until half an hour before you want to cook it.

Meanwhile, make an orange syrup by heating the sugar with the orange juice in a small pan until dissolved. Add the orange peel julienne and simmer on a low heat for about 20 minutes or until syrupy; remove from the heat and set aside. At the same time, crush the saffron lightly in a pestle and mortar, then put into a saucepan with 250ml water and bring to the boil; remove from the heat and leave to infuse.

When you are ready to cook the rice, heat the butter and oil in a wok and fry the spices with the shallots and bay leaf for about 30 seconds, making sure the butter does not burn. Drain the rice and add to the wok. Toss quickly so the rice grains become coated with the spicy butter. Transfer the contents of the wok to a rice cooker and shake it so that the rice is uniformly level. Pour in the saffron water and add enough extra water to come about 8mm above the surface of the rice. Steam the rice for 10–12 minutes, or according to the rice cooker's instructions, until the rice is tender. If you don't have a rice cooker you can use a large saucepan.

Add the candied orange peel julienne and a tablespoon of the orange syrup to the rice and stir in with a fork, then fluff up the grains. Remove the large spices and bay leaf before eating.

For the chips. Peel the potatoes and cut lengthways into 2cm slices. Cut each slice lengthways into neat, thick chips. Put them into a colander and rinse under cold water to remove excess starch. Part-cook in a pan of boiling water for 5–8 minutes or until just tender. Using a strainer or slotted spoon, remove the chips from the pan and spread them out on a baking tray. Leave to dry and cool.

Heat oil for deep-frying to 130°C. Add the chips and deep-fry for 3–4 minutes or until cooked through but not browned. Remove the chips from the pan with a slotted spoon and drain on kitchen paper. Cool.

Just before serving, heat the oil for deep-frying again, to 180°C this time, and fry the chips until golden and crisp. Drain and sprinkle with salt, then keep hot.

For the duck. Preheat the oven to 170°C/Gas Mark 3$\frac{1}{2}$. Score the skin on the duck breasts and season with salt. Lay the breasts skin side down in a cold ovenproof frying pan and set on a medium-high heat. Fry for about 5 minutes or until the skin is golden brown. Turn the breasts over and brown the other side for 2 minutes. Transfer the pan to the oven to finish cooking for 5 minutes. Remove the duck breasts and leave to rest for 15 minutes. (While the breasts are resting you can finish the curry sauce and give the chips their second frying.)

To serve. Pour the curry sauce into the centre of each plate in a perfect circle. Cut the duck breasts across in half and arrange on the sauce. Scatter coriander shoots on top of the duck. Serve the rice and chips with the curry.

PAN-FRIED DUCK BREAST, CONFIT DUCK SPRING ROLL, PAK CHOI, SWEET POTATO PURÉE
AND A STAR ANISE CARAMEL DRESSING SERVES 4

Duck lends itself towards sweeter flavours. Here, I've put it with different levels of sweetness in every other part of the dish, from the delicate pak choi to the rich caramel dressing. The duck breasts should be cooked medium.

4 small pak choi, each cut lengthways
in half
1 tablespoon olive oil
4 duck breasts

For the confit duck legs
30g rock salt
2 fresh bay leaves, finely sliced
4 garlic cloves, finely sliced
1 tablespoon coriander seeds, crushed
1 tablespoon black peppercorns, crushed
2 duck legs
800g duck fat

For the caramel dressing
100g caster sugar
6 star anise
200ml chicken stock

For the spring rolls
2 tablespoons hoisin sauce
4 sheets of filo pastry
oil for deep-frying

For the sweet potato purée
2 medium sweet potatoes, peeled
25g butter
25–50ml double cream
salt and pepper to taste

For the confit duck legs. The night before, combine the salt and all the aromatics (bay leaves, garlic, coriander seeds and peppercorns) in a large bowl. Add the duck legs and turn to coat with the mixture, really pushing the salt into them. Cover the bowl with clingfilm and leave in the fridge for 12 hours.

The next day, brush the salt mix off the duck legs. Put the duck fat into a flameproof casserole and bring the fat up to a gentle, bubbling simmer. Place the duck legs in the fat and leave to cook very gently for 2^1/$_2$–3 hours. Take the confit legs out of the fat and, when cool, remove the meat from the bones. Shred the meat and reserve for the spring rolls.

For the caramel dressing. While the duck legs are confiting, put the sugar and 100ml water in a saucepan and cook to a golden caramel. Add the star anise and chicken stock and stir to mix, then leave on a low heat for 1 hour. Strain and reserve.

For the spring rolls. Mix the shredded duck with the hoisin sauce. Divide among the sheets of filo pastry and roll up, tucking in the sides, to make four spring rolls. Set aside until ready to fry.

Before serving, heat oil for deep-frying to 170°C, then deep-fry the spring rolls until golden all over. Drain on kitchen paper and keep hot.

For the sweet potato purée. Cook the sweet potatoes in a pan of boiling salted water for 10–15 minutes or until tender. Drain well, then return to the pan and heat for a few seconds to drive off any excess moisture. Transfer the sweet potatoes to a blender and add half of the butter and cream. Blend until smooth, adding more butter and cream if you like, and seasoning to taste. Set aside in a pan, ready to reheat for serving.

For the pak choi. Cook the pak choi in a pan of boiling salted water for 2 minutes. Drain and reserve. Before serving, fry in a frying pan with some olive oil until lightly browned and heated through.

For the duck breasts. Preheat the oven to 200°C/Gas Mark 6. Score the skin on the duck breasts, then place them skin side down in a cold frying pan. Set on a medium heat and fry until the skin is golden. Turn the breasts over and continue cooking for 2 minutes. Transfer the breasts to a baking tray and place in the oven to finish cooking for 8–10 minutes. Allow to rest in a warm place for 5 minutes.

To serve. Spoon the sweet potato purée on to the plates. Cut the duck breasts diagonally in half and place, cut side up, on the purée. Add the pak choi and spring rolls to the plates and spoon the star anise caramel around the plate. Finish with a sprinkle of freshly ground black pepper.

One of my favourite dishes
of all time.

APPLE PIE AND RHUBARB ICE CREAM

SERVES 4

One of my favourite dishes of all time is apple pie – sweet, sour and so moreish.
Rhubarb ice cream is perfect with this one.

For the rhubarb ice cream
500g rhubarb, roughly chopped
250g caster sugar
seeds from 1 vanilla pod
300ml double cream

For the apple pies
600g Bramley apples, peeled, cored and
   sliced
2 tablespoons lemon juice
100g caster sugar, plus extra for sprinkling
1 tablespoon ground cinnamon
25g unsalted butter, cut into small pieces
2 tablespoons cornflour
1 packet (about 350g) puff pastry, thawed
   if frozen
1 egg, lightly beaten with a dash of milk,
   for egg wash

For the rhubarb ice cream. Put the rhubarb into a saucepan with the sugar and vanilla seeds and cook on a medium heat for about 15 minutes or until soft and broken down. Pass through a fine sieve into a bowl and allow to cool.

Whip the cream until it will form soft peaks. Transfer to an ice cream machine and start the churning process, then slowly pour in the cooled rhubarb purée. Once all is incorporated, leave to churn according to the manufacturer's instructions. When ready, transfer the ice cream to a freezer container and keep in the freezer until needed.

For the apple pies. Preheat the oven to 200°C/Gas Mark 6. For the apple pie filling, mix together the apples, lemon juice, sugar, cinnamon, butter and cornflour in a mixing bowl. Divide among four large ramekins or small casserole dishes and set these on a baking tray. Place in the oven to soften for 20 minutes. Remove and allow to cool. Leave the oven on.

While the apple filling is cooling, roll out the puff pastry on a lightly floured work surface and cut out four discs to make lids for the ramekins or casserole dishes. Lay these on a tray and keep in the fridge until needed.

Brush the rim of each ramekin with egg wash, then cover it with a pastry disc, pressing the pastry to the rim to seal. Brush the pastry with egg wash. Place in the oven and bake for about 18 minutes or until the pastry is puffed up and golden.

To serve. Sprinkle the hot apple pies with caster sugar, then serve with scoops of rhubarb ice cream.

POACHED PEAR AND STEM GINGER ICE CREAM WITH CANDIED HAZELNUTS   SERVES 4

The pear poached in dessert wine with star anise gives this dish a rich feel, and the candied hazelnuts provide a nice textural dimension. What's not to like?

For the ginger ice cream
4 large egg yolks
25g caster sugar
300ml double cream
4 pieces of stem ginger, cut into small cubes
2 tablespoons ginger syrup from the jar

For the candied hazelnuts
12 hazelnuts, toasted and skinned
200g caster sugar

For the poached pears
4 ripe but firm Conference pears
600ml dessert wine
200ml orange juice
juice of 1 lemon
400g caster sugar
2 star anise
1 vanilla pod, split open

To garnish
edible violas
star anise

For the ginger ice cream. Put the egg yolks and sugar in a bowl and whisk together until pale and thickened. In a separate bowl whip the cream to soft peaks. Add the cream to the whisked mixture along with the ginger and ginger syrup and mix together thoroughly. Pour into an ice cream machine and churn according to the manufacturer's instructions. Transfer to a freezerproof container and keep in the freezer until needed. (If the ice cream becomes too firm, let it soften a bit at room temperature before serving.)

For the candied hazelnuts. Gently insert the pointed end of a long wooden skewer into the side of each hazelnut. Place a cutting board along the edge of a work surface; lay newspaper on the floor, directly under the cutting board.

Dissolve the sugar in 175ml water in a heavy saucepan over medium heat, stirring occasionally. When the syrup is clear stop stirring and cook until the syrup comes to the boil, washing down the sides of the pan with a wet pastry brush to prevent crystals from forming. Boil, gently swirling the syrup occasionally, until the caramel is a medium amber. Remove from the heat and leave for about 10 minutes or until thickened. (To test, dip a skewer in the caramel and lift it up 7cm or so – if a thick drip slowly forms and holds a string, the caramel is ready to use.)

Dip a skewered hazelnut into the caramel and lift out, letting excess caramel drip back into the pan. When the dripping caramel becomes a thin string, secure the opposite end of the skewer under the cutting board (so the hazelnut is suspended over the newspaper). Repeat with the remaining hazelnuts. If the caramel hardens before all the hazelnuts have been dipped, rewarm it over low heat. Leave to cool for about 5 minutes or until the caramel string has hardened, then break each string to the desired length. Carefully remove the skewers.

For the poached pears. Peel the pears. Combine the wine, orange and lemon juices, caster sugar, star anise and vanilla pod in a large saucepan and heat, stirring, until the sugar dissolves. Add the pears to the saucepan – they should be covered with liquid, so lay a round of baking parchment on top to keep them submerged. Bring to the boil, then simmer gently for 5 minutes or until the pears are tender. Remove from the heat and leave the pears in the syrup to cool (serve them at room temperature).

To serve. Remove the pears from the syrup, then take a slice off the bottom of each one so it has a flat surface to stand on. Stand a pear on each plate. Put a quenelle of ice cream next to the pear and garnish with one viola. Add candied hazelnuts and a star anise, if you wish.

My take on a classic dessert.

LEMON TART

SERVES 8

FROM THE SERIES

Once into the Semi-Finals, I was tasked with cooking dessert for the Bond Girls at the Savoy Hotel. It seemed fitting to go for something as timeless and utterly gorgeous as this lemon tart.

For the pastry
250g plain flour
150g unsalted butter
50g icing sugar, sifted
1 egg
beaten egg, for brushing

For the filling
6 eggs
300g caster sugar
250ml double cream
200ml lemon juice

For the raspberry coulis
250g raspberries
200g caster sugar
a squeeze of lemon juice

To garnish
20g icing sugar
rose petals or other edible flowers

For the pastry. Combine the flour, butter and sugar in a bowl and rub together until the mixture looks like breadcrumbs. Mix in the egg and knead briefly to bring together into a pastry dough. Don't overwork the dough. Shape into a ball, wrap in clingfilm and leave to rest in the fridge for 30 minutes.

Preheat the oven to 160°C/Gas Mark 3. Press the ball of dough on a lightly floured surface to flatten it. Dust with a pinch of flour, then roll out to the thickness of a pound coin. Use to line a 28cm flan ring set on a baking tray, or a loose-bottomed tart tin. Line the pastry case with baking parchment and fill with baking beans. Bake blind for 15 minutes.

Remove the baking beans and paper, then bake for a further 5 minutes. Remove from the oven. Brush the inside of the pastry case with beaten egg, then allow to cool. Leave the oven on, but reduce the temperature to 120°C/Gas Mark 1/2.

For the filling. Whisk the eggs and caster sugar together in a bowl just to mix. Add the cream and lemon juice. Pour into a heavy-based saucepan and heat gently, stirring, until the mixture reaches 38°C. Transfer to a measuring jug.

Set the baking tray or tart tin on the partially pulled-out oven rack. Pour the filling into the pastry case, then carefully slide the rack into the oven. Bake for 35 minutes or until the filling is set but still slightly wobbly in the centre (the temperature in the centre should be 70°C). Remove the tart from the oven and leave to cool for at least 1 1/2 hours so that the filling can set.

For the raspberry coulis. Put the raspberries in a saucepan and add the sugar and lemon juice. Cook gently until you have a consistency just short of a jam. It should coat the back of a spoon. Pass through a fine sieve into a bowl. Set aside.

To serve. Dust the whole tart with sifted icing sugar, then cut into neat wedges. Place one in the middle of each plate. Using a teaspoon, drizzle the raspberry coulis around the tart. Garnish with rose petals.

SANGRIA
(FRUIT WITH ORANGE JELLY AND RED WINE JUS)
SERVES 4

I rather adore desserts based around alcohol (see my MasterChef Final recipe on the following page). This is a dessert of such simplicity, but it really delivers.

1 Cox's apple, cut into 8 wedges
   and cored
segments from 1 grapefruit

For the orange jelly
grated zest of 1 orange
80g caster sugar
400ml freshly squeezed orange juice
juice of 1 lemon
1 sachet powdered gelatine

For the red wine jus
750ml red wine (Rioja)
1 vanilla pod
300g caster sugar
grated zest and juice of 3 oranges
1 gelatine leaf

For the orange jelly. Put the orange zest in a small bowl. Heat the sugar with 4 tablespoons water in a small pan until dissolved, then pour the resulting syrup over the zest and leave to cool. Combine the orange and lemon juices in another bowl. Dissolve the gelatine in 4 tablespoons of hot water; when smooth, pour it into the fruit juice. Strain in the sugar syrup. Mix well. Pour into a clingfilm-lined 20cm square shallow tray. Place in the fridge and leave for several hours, or overnight, to set.

For the red wine jus. Pour the red wine into a pan, bring to the boil and boil for 1 minute. Add the remaining jus ingredients, except the gelatine leaf, and bring back to a simmer.

Add the apples to the red wine jus and poach gently for 10 minutes. Meanwhile, soak the gelatine leaf in cold water for about 2 minutes to soften. Remove the apples with a slotted spoon and reserve. Squeeze excess liquid from the gelatine leaf, then add to the red wine jus and stir until melted. Leave to cool to room temperature.

To serve. Cut the orange jelly into four 4cm cubes and place one in each serving bowl. Set poached apple wedges and grapefruit segments on the jelly and spoon around the red wine jus.

Fruit and wine – so simple.

CHOCOLATE MOJITO SERVES 4

FROM THE SERIES,
FINAL DISH

It was only fitting that I closed off the show with a drink-based dessert, although there's much more going on here than just alcohol: sweetness, sharpness and bitterness, and a variety of textures and temperatures. Cheers!

For the mojito snow
50g sugar
leaves from a bunch of mint
juice of 3 limes
3 tablespoons white rum

For the Thai basil gel
leaves from a bunch of basil
leaves from a bunch of Thai basil
65g sugar
2g agar agar

For the chocolate cylinder
200g dark chocolate (with 70% cocoa
   solids), broken up

For the coconut crumble
25g almond flour
75g unsalted butter, softened
50g desiccated coconut
30g caster sugar
50g plain flour
1 egg plus 1 yolk

For the caramel sauce
125g caster sugar
130ml double cream

For the candied cucumber
1 cucumber
100g caster sugar

edible red rose, to garnish

For the mojito snow. Dissolve the sugar in 350ml water in a saucepan. Add the mint leaves and heat up slightly but do not bring to the boil or the mint will go brown. Add the lime juice. Lift out the mint leaves, squeezing the liquid from the leaves back into the pan. Pass the liquid through muslin into a jug. Stir in the rum. Pour the mixture into a shallow, wide freezerproof container.

Using a blast chiller, freeze for 2 hours, breaking up the granita with a fork every half hour. Alternatively freeze for about 6 hours in a regular freezer. Put the frozen granita into a blender and blitz it to a consistency that resembles snow. Keep in the freezer until needed. When ready to serve, fill four shot glasses, or other small glasses, with the snow.

For the Thai basil gel. Blanch all the basil leaves in a pan of boiling water for 3 seconds, then quickly scoop out using a sieve and plunge into iced water. Set aside in the water for 5 minutes. Drain the basil and put into a small food processor. Blitz to a purée. Set aside.

Mix the sugar and agar agar with 150ml cold water in a small pan. Bring to the boil, then remove from the heat and cool. When almost set, slowly add the basil purée while blending with a hand blender. The resulting gel should be liquid in consistency but not runny. Set aside.

For the chocolate cylinders. Put a third of the chocolate into a heatproof bowl set over a pan of gently simmering water. Heat the chocolate to melt it. When it reaches 48°C, remove the bowl from the pan and add the remaining chocolate. Stir until all the chocolate is melted and smooth. Leave to cool to 32°C.

For each cylinder, use an offset spatula to spread chocolate in an even layer on a 10 x 15cm acetate sheet. Gently form the acetate, with the chocolate inside, into a cylinder. Put into a 4cm diameter pipe mould or ring to hold the cylinder in shape. Leave to cool and set.

For the coconut crumble. Preheat the oven to 180°C/Gas Mark 4. Line a baking tray with baking parchment. In a bowl, beat the almond flour, butter, coconut, caster sugar, flour, whole egg and egg yolk together with a wooden spoon until well mixed to a dough. Using your fingers, take little nuggets of the dough, pressing them gently together, and place on the lined baking tray. Bake for about 10 minutes or until set, golden and crumbly. Leave to cool.

For the caramel sauce. Dissolve the caster sugar in 2 tablespoons water in a pan, then cook to form a medium caramel. Remove from the heat and stir in 70ml of the cream until smooth.

Using an electric mixer, whisk the remaining cream until slightly thickened but not to the point of forming soft peaks. Whisk the whipped cream into the caramel. Keep in the fridge until needed.

For the candied cucumber. Using a vegetable peeler, take four wide lengthways strips from the cucumber (don't use the first strip, which will be mainly skin – each strip should have skin on the sides). Put the sugar and 100ml water in a vacuum bag and add the cucumber strips. Seal and compress. If you don't have a vacuum-pack machine you can use a plastic food bag, with the air pressed out before sealing. Leave to marinate for about 2 hours.

To serve. Make a 'swoosh' of caramel sauce on each plate. Set a mojito shot glass in the centre. Carefully remove the acetate from a chocolate cylinder, then place next to the shot glass. Put drops of Thai basil gel around the plate using a teaspoon. Garnish with the rolled-up candied cucumber. Add random pieces of coconut crumble on the plate. Finish with a few rose petals.

CHOCOLATE SOUFFLÉ AND VANILLA CREAM

SERVES 4

FROM THE SERIES

After all the trouble I had with this, I thought that I never wanted to see a soufflé again! But I've changed my mind. I still love this one.

For the chocolate soufflé
soft unsalted butter and caster sugar for the dishes
150g dark chocolate (with 70% cocoa solids), broken into small pieces
6 egg whites
125g caster sugar
icing sugar, for dusting

For the vanilla cream
300ml single cream
2 vanilla pods, split open

For the chocolate soufflé. Using a pastry brush, cover the insides of four medium-sized (about 100ml) ramekins with a layer of soft butter. On the sides make sure the strokes of butter go upwards to form 'tramlines', which will help the soufflés to rise. Coat the buttered insides with sugar, shaking out the excess. Place the ramekins in the fridge to set the butter.

Preheat the oven to 180°C/Gas Mark 4. Put the chocolate in a heatproof bowl set over a pan of simmering water and melt, stirring occasionally. Remove from the pan of water and reserve. Combine the egg whites with a third of the sugar in another heatproof bowl and set over the same pan of simmering water. Whisk for 2–3 minutes or until doubled in volume. Remove the bowl from the pan and whisk in the rest of the sugar until the mixture will form soft peaks.

Spoon a third of the egg white mix into the melted chocolate and whisk together. Carefully fold in the rest of the egg white mix, just until there are no streaks. Fill the prepared ramekins with the mixture and smooth off the tops. Bake for 20–25 minutes or until risen (make the vanilla cream while the soufflés are in the oven). Remove and serve immediately.

For the vanilla cream. Warm the cream in a saucepan over a medium heat for about 3 minutes, without boiling. Meanwhile, scrape the seeds from the vanilla pods using the back of a knife. Add the seeds to the cream and set aside to infuse for at least 5 minutes (serve warm or cold).

To serve. Pour the vanilla cream into four little jugs. Set a ramekin on each plate and place a jug of vanilla cream next to it. Dust the top of the soufflé with sifted icing sugar.

You'll want to lick the bowl clean.

When creating dishes I always start with a single ingredient
that I want to showcase. From this point, I paint a picture of
what the end result should be. Quite often, a dish will need
tweaking, perhaps as many as three or four times to perfect
each component.

With each of my recipes in this book you will be able to add
your own twists and turns to make them just as you like
them. I like the challenge of exploring the food of different
countries and cultures, and so you'll see influences from
French, Italian, British, Indian and even Thai cuisine for
you to try at home.

My signature recipe is the Chicken Burger (page 194) while
the Chilli Crab Noodles (page 184) and Chocolate Truffle Cake
(page 226) are two of my personal favourites. As for my mum
– my biggest supporter and first-choice critic – she adores
my Sea Bass, Citrus Fruits and Samphire with Braised Fennel
(page 160)! I really hope you enjoy reliving my TV dishes,
and that you love trying some of my new recipes, which
are a mix of new experiments and old favourites.

SEA BASS, CITRUS FRUITS AND SAMPHIRE WITH BRAISED FENNEL SERVES 2

I know it sounds like a peculiar combination, but this was the first plate of food of my own design that the judges tasted and it went down a storm. With a fresh zingy vinaigrette, light pan-fried fish and the textures of fennel and samphire, it makes the perfect starter before a meaty main course.

For the fennel
1 bulb of fennel
50g unsalted butter
500ml chicken stock

For the citrus fruits and vinaigrette
1 ripe ruby-red grapefruit
1 ripe white grapefruit
3 oranges
juice of 1 lemon
about 150ml extra virgin olive oil
2 tablespoons golden caster sugar,
    or to taste

For the sea bass and samphire
2 whole fillets of sea bass
    (preferably wild sea bass)
olive oil
a knob of unsalted butter
50g samphire
juice of 1 lemon
salt and white pepper to taste

For the fennel. Pick off the fennel fronds and set aside for the garnish. Peel the outer leaves off the bulb and trim the root. Cut the bulb lengthways in half and then into quarters.

Heat a heavy-based saucepan with the butter, add the fennel quarters and brown on a high heat for 4–5 minutes on each side. Add the stock. Cover the pan, reduce the heat and braise for 8–12 minutes or until the fennel is soft when pierced with a knife. Once the fennel is cooked, remove the pan from the heat and keep warm.

For the citrus fruits and vinaigrette. While the fennel is cooking, peel the grapefruits and one of the oranges, then cut out the segments from the membrane. Squeeze the juice from the other oranges and pour into a small saucepan. Bring to the boil and reduce by half. Add the lemon juice and measure the liquid, then add the same quantity of olive oil (you may not need all the oil). Season to taste with sugar, salt and white pepper. Set the vinaigrette aside with the citrus segments.

For the sea bass and samphire. Cut each fillet into three equal pieces, then score the skin of each piece. Heat a frying pan and add a little olive oil. Season the fillets on the skin side, then place skin side down in the pan and sear, without moving them, for 4–6 minutes. Season the flesh side and flip the fillets over. Add the butter to the pan. Cook the fillets for a further minute, spooning the foaming butter over them. Remove and keep warm.

Add the samphire to the pan and cook for a few minutes to soften. Season and add the lemon juice.

To serve. Place the fennel quarters on the plates and rest three pieces of sea bass up against or on top of the fennel in a line. Arrange the fruit segments around the plate, then add the samphire in between each piece of fish. Spoon over the vinaigrette and dress the sea bass with the fennel fronds.

Fish with fruit... try it – you'll love it!

PAN-FRIED HAKE, SPINACH PURÉE, KALE, CHARGRILLED BROCCOLI AND PESTO   SERVES 4

This is the first meal I ever cooked for my partner. It's hassle-free, looks pretty as a picture and is beautifully fresh and vibrant. While it's quick, easy and healthy, it looks really rather impressive (I got a second date!). It has become one of our favourites and we eat it regularly during the week when time is against us. You can use other green vegetables in season – asparagus, spring greens, courgettes, broad beans or whatever you like – and other white fish, such as cod, pollock or sea bass.

4 fillets of hake (skin on)
olive oil, for frying
a squeeze of lemon juice
extra virgin olive oil, to finish
salt and black and white pepper to taste

For the pesto
75g basil leaves
25g flat-leaf parsley leaves
2 garlic cloves, peeled
2 tablespoons pine nuts
about 100ml olive oil

For the spinach purée
1 banana shallot, finely sliced
olive oil, for frying
400g spinach
100ml chicken stock

For the broccoli and kale
1 head of broccoli
12 garlic cloves, peeled
200g curly kale
olive oil, for frying
grated zest and juice of 1 lemon

For the pesto. Put the basil and parsley leaves in a blender with the garlic and pine nuts. Blitz to a coarse crumb texture. With the motor running, slowly add the olive oil through the feed tube until the pesto has a sauce-like consistency (you may not need all the olive oil). Taste the pesto and season with salt and black pepper; taste again and adjust if necessary. When you are happy with the taste, put the pesto in a jar and keep in the fridge until needed.

For the spinach purée. Fry the shallot in a little olive oil in a saucepan big enough to hold all of the spinach. When the shallot is soft and translucent (don't let it brown) add the spinach and stir until it has wilted (it will reduce to a fifth of its volume) – this will only take a couple of minutes. Immediately add the stock to the pan and season with salt and white pepper. Transfer the mixture to a blender and pulse to a purée. Pass this through a sieve into a clean pan. You should have a bright green, smooth, soup-like consistency. Taste the purée and add more salt or white pepper if you think it needs it. Set aside, ready to reheat gently when needed.

For the broccoli. Prepare the broccoli by trimming the stem at the base, removing about 5mm right around the base with a small knife or vegetable peeler. Stand the head of broccoli on its end and slice it straight down in half and then in half again into large quarters. Cook in a pan of lightly salted water for about 5 minutes or until slightly softened but still a little bit hard at the base. Remove (reserve the pan of water) and refresh in cold water, then set aside.

For the kale. Bring the pan of water back to the boil, then drop in the whole garlic cloves. Boil for 1 minute. Remove with a slotted spoon and cool in iced water for 1 minute. Repeat this blanching process three times, using the same pan of boiling water. Set the garlic aside.

Using a steamer, steam the kale for 4–5 minutes or until tender. In a clean pan, heat a small amount of olive oil, add the blanched garlic and fry for 2–3 minutes. Add the kale and season with a little salt, some white pepper, the lemon zest and a generous squeeze of lemon juice. Mix well. Remove from the heat and set aside, covered, ready to reheat when needed.

For the hake. Preheat the oven to 170°C/ Gas Mark 3¹/₂. To prepare the fish, check for any bones and dry the skin completely with kitchen paper. Heat an ovenproof frying pan on the hob, add some olive oil and heat until very hot. Season the fish on its skin side, then place skin side down in the pan. Turn the heat down slightly and cook the fish for 4–5 minutes or until you can see that the flesh is turning from opaque to white – don't be tempted to move the fish or the skin will break.

Season the flesh side with salt and white pepper. When the top of the fish is nearly white, flip the fillets over and sprinkle with a squeeze of lemon juice. Immediately transfer the pan to the oven and cook for 3–4 minutes or until the fish is perfectly cooked (you need to check it like steak – if it feels springy with a little give when you poke it then it's cooked; if it's soft it needs a bit longer; if it's really firm then it's overcooked!). Remove from the oven, lift the fish on to a clean plate and leave to rest for 5 minutes.

To finish the broccoli and kale. While the fish is resting, heat a ridged griddle pan until smoking hot, then add a very small amount of olive oil and place the broccoli, on a cut side, in the pan. Leave it without moving for at least 3–4 minutes – you want the broccoli to get charred lines. Then turn it on to its other cut side and repeat. While the broccoli is being chargrilled, gently reheat the spinach purée and the kale.

To serve. Spoon the spinach purée into the centre of four shallow serving bowls. Add a quarter of charred broccoli and some kale with two cloves of garlic. Gently place the hake alongside, skin side up. Dress with a few teaspoons of pesto and a drizzle of extra virgin olive oil.

DOVER SOLE EN PAPILLOTE WITH JULIENNE OF FENNEL, NEW ZEALAND CLAMS AND A THAI BASIL PESTO SERVES 4

There's something very unassuming about this dish. I know that when I announced I was going to make fish en papillote for 12 food critics, a few eyebrows were raised, but my girlfriend, who is my biggest fan and chief taster (her opinion is as good as any, in my book), gave it her vote. Playing safe might have been the order of the day, but it's not me. I was true to myself in every round of the competition and was prepared to be bold and daring. So I took a risk. I wanted to design a memorable three-course menu and this dish was the starter. It booked my place in the Final.

12 fresh New Zealand littleneck clams
  (or 24 smaller fresh clams)
1 lemon, ends trimmed and cut into
  4 discs
4 large whole fillets of Dover sole, skinned
1 mild red chilli, finely sliced
butter
4 tablespoons Pinot Grigio wine

For the pesto
leaves from a small bunch of Thai basil
leaves from a small bunch of flat-leaf
  parsley
100ml olive oil
1 garlic clove, peeled

For the vegetables
1 tablespoon olive oil
2 bulbs of baby fennel, cut into julienne
4 small baby leeks, cut into julienne
100g sugar snaps, cut into julienne
2 garlic cloves, finely sliced
20–24 cherry tomatoes on the vine,
  cut into 4 sprigs
salt and pepper to taste

For the pesto. Reserve 1 heaped tablespoon each of the Thai basil and parsley leaves for the garnish and put the rest in a mini food processor with the olive oil and garlic. Blitz to a coarse sauce-like consistency. Season well. Transfer to a bowl and set aside.

For the clams. Put the clams in a bowl of cold water and leave them for 20 minutes to clean themselves of any sand. Lift them from the water (do not drain) and place in a clean bowl. Set aside.

For the vegetables. Preheat the oven to 220°C/Gas Mark 7. Heat the olive oil in a large frying pan, add the julienned vegetables and garlic, and soften for 2 minutes. Remove from the heat and set aside.

Season the tomatoes and place on a small baking tray. Roast for 5–10 minutes or until slightly softened. Remove from the oven and set aside. Leave the oven on.

For the lemon slices. Heat a ridged griddle pan over a medium heat and chargrill the lemon slices for about 4 minutes or until caramelised on each side. Remove and set aside.

For the parcels. Cut out four 30cm rounds of baking parchment. Fold each round in half to create a crease, then open up again. For each parcel, place a tablespoon of pesto on one side of the paper round, near the centre of the crease. Cut a sole fillet lengthways in half. Season each strip of fish, then put a tablespoon of the julienned vegetables near the thicker end and roll up. Set the two rolls on the pesto. Place the clams next to the rolled sole and top with a sprig of roasted tomatoes, a few slices of chilli, a caramelised lemon slice and a small knob of butter. Finish with a sprinkle of the reserved Thai basil and parsley, and season well. Fold the other side of the paper round over to create a half moon and crimp the edges to seal, leaving a 2.5cm gap right at the end. Add a tablespoon of white wine into the gap, then seal it.

Place the parcels on a baking tray and bake for 10 minutes or until they have puffed up; the fish will be cooked and the clams will have steamed open.

To serve. Place the unopened parcels on the plates and leave each diner to pierce his parcel and take in the aromas before eating.

Making Dover Sole en Papillote with Julienne of Fennel, New Zealand Clams and a Thai Basil Pesto (see page 164).

SMOKED COD WITH A MUSSEL AND VEGETABLE BROTH, ANCHOVY PUFFS AND PESTO SERVES 4

FROM THE SERIES

This dish brings back memories of time spent in France in the Dordogne region. My parents would take us on a 15-hour car journey from Cardiff to Sarlat, stopping along the way to sample some of France's best food. You can prepare the anchovy puffs, pesto and broth in advance, then reheat and pan-fry the fish at the last minute.

4 pieces of undyed smoked cod fillet, about 200g each
25g unsalted butter
olive oil, for frying
salt and white pepper to taste

For the broth
3 tablespoons olive oil
1 small leek, sliced
1 white onion, roughly chopped
2 garlic cloves, sliced
1 small carrot, diced
1 waxy potato, diced
1 turnip, diced
a piece of Parmesan rind (if available)
3 baby courgettes, diced
a handful of fat green beans
a handful of shelled and skinned broad beans (fresh or frozen)
2 very ripe, large vine tomatoes, peeled, deseeded and finely diced

For the pesto
a large bunch of basil
1 garlic clove, peeled
50ml extra virgin olive oil

For the anchovy puffs
500g all-butter ready-rolled puff pastry (1 sheet), thawed if frozen
100g fresh marinated anchovy fillets, drained
50g capers in brine, drained and rinsed
3 tablespoons chopped parsley
1 egg, beaten

For the mussels
a knob of butter
1 shallot, diced
1 garlic clove, finely sliced
50ml white wine

20 fresh mussels, scrubbed and debearded
a few sprigs of parsley, finely chopped
1 teaspoon lemon juice

For the broth. Heat the olive oil in a large shallow pan and sweat the leek, onion, garlic, carrot, potato and turnip all together for 5 minutes or until starting to soften. Add the Parmesan rind and cover with water. Bring to the boil, then simmer for 5 minutes. Add the courgettes and green beans and simmer for a further 5 minutes, topping up the water if necessary, until all the vegetables are soft but still retain some bite. Add the broad beans. Bring back to the boil and season well, then remove from the heat. Set aside, ready to reheat for serving.

For the pesto. Blend all the ingredients together in a small blender until a smooth paste is formed. (You may not need all the oil – you don't want the pesto to be too thin.) Keep in the fridge until needed.

For the anchovy puffs. Preheat the oven to 220°C/Gas Mark 7. Lay the sheet of puff pastry on a very lightly floured surface. Arrange the anchovies side by side on the diagonal across the top half of the pastry. Season with white pepper and add a sprinkle of capers and chopped parsley. Cut off the bottom half of the puff pastry sheet and place this over the anchovies on the top half, matching all the edges and corners. Press the edges to seal. Cut the pastry lengthways into four long strips and twist each of them a couple of times. Brush them with beaten egg,

then place on a baking sheet lined with greaseproof paper. Bake for 10 minutes. Flip the puffs over and brush the other side with beaten egg. Bake for a further 10 minutes or until golden and puffed up. While the puffs are baking, prepare the mussels and cod.

For the mussels. Melt the butter in a deep pan and soften the shallot and garlic. Add the white wine and boil to reduce by half. Add the mussels, cover the pan and steam for 3 minutes or until the mussels have opened. Stir in the parsley. Drain the mussels in a sieve set over a clean pan; keep the mussels warm. Boil the cooking liquid over a high heat to reduce to about 2 tablespoons. Taste and adjust the seasoning, adding the lemon juice to finish, then stir into the broth.

For the smoked cod. Pan-fry the cod fillets in hot butter and oil in a pan for 4–5 minutes on one side or until golden. Flip them over and cook for a further minute. Remove from the heat.

To serve. Remove eight mussels from their shells and add them to the broth. Gently reheat the broth, adding the tomatoes and pesto to taste. Serve the broth in deep bowls, placing the cod in the centre. Put an anchovy puff and three mussels in their shells on the side of each bowl. Add a final drizzle of pesto and serve.

One of my all-time favourite entertaining dishes.

I love the comfort of a warming spiced curry.

COD LOIN WITH FRAGRANT CURRY SAUCE AND CORIANDER RICE **SERVES 4**

There are two occasions in particular when I crave curry: when there is sport on TV, and when I'm nursing a sore head! Some of the best curries take a long time to prepare, but you can also make an array of curries in less time if you use fish rather than a slow-cook meat cut like lamb shoulder. This curry has the perfect balance of spice and fragrance without overpowering the delicate nature of the white fish.

4 skinless, boneless portions of cod loin, about 175g each

For the naan breads
450g white bread flour
2 teaspoons salt
1 teaspoon fast-action dried yeast
175ml lukewarm water
2 tablespoons sunflower oil
1 teaspoon honey
4 tablespoons plain yoghurt
4 garlic cloves, peeled
4 tablespoons ghee, melted
4 tablespoons chopped coriander

For the rice
2 tablespoons groundnut oil
1 teaspoon coriander seeds
2 kaffir lime leaves, finely shredded
250g basmati rice, cooked and cooled
2 tablespoons chopped coriander

For the curry sauce
3 tablespoons vegetable oil
1 teaspoon black mustard seeds
4 bay leaves
4 banana shallots, finely sliced
4 garlic cloves, sliced
1 tablespoon grated fresh ginger
1 green chilli, finely sliced
1 tablespoon chilli powder
1 teaspoon ground turmeric
1 x 400ml can coconut milk
1 x 400g can tomatoes
salt and pepper to taste

To finish the sauce
2 tablespoons double cream

2 ripe tomatoes, thickly sliced
4 tablespoons chopped coriander
juice of ½ lime

For the naan breads. Sift the flour and 1 teaspoon salt into a large mixing bowl and stir in the yeast. Add the lukewarm water and mix together with your hands. Add the oil, honey and yoghurt and mix to make a dough. Cover the bowl with a damp tea towel and leave in a warm place to rise for about 1 hour or until doubled in size.

Turn out the dough on to a well-floured surface and knock it back before dividing equally into four portions. Using your hands, stretch and pull each portion into a large flattened oval shape. Lightly grease two baking trays with vegetable oil. Lay the naans on the trays, cover with a warm, dry tea towel and leave to rise in a warm place for about 20 minutes or until doubled in size.

While you wait for the breads to rise, preheat the grill to medium–high. Finely chop the garlic with the remaining 1 teaspoon salt to make a paste, then mix in the hot melted ghee; set aside.

When the bread is ready, lightly spray each naan with water using a mister, then grill for 6–8 minutes on each side or until browned. Remove from the heat. While they are still hot, brush one side of the naan with the garlic ghee, then sprinkle with chopped coriander.

(If you want to make the naan breads in advance, reheat them in a low oven for 5–6 minutes before serving.)

For the rice. Heat a saucepan and add the oil and coriander seeds. Fry the seeds for 2–3 minutes or until they pop. Add the kaffir lime leaves and cook for a further 2–3 minutes, then add the cooked rice and coriander. Toss well to mix the rice with the flavourings. Set aside, ready to reheat for serving.

For the curry sauce. Heat a large frying pan and add the vegetable oil, mustard seeds and bay leaves. Gently cook for 2–3 minutes to release the aromas before adding the shallots, garlic, ginger and green chilli. Continue cooking gently for 5 minutes, stirring. Mix the chilli powder and turmeric with 1 teaspoon water to make a paste. Add this to the pan and cook for a further minute. Add the coconut milk along with the canned tomatoes, and season with salt and pepper. Bring to the boil, then simmer for 5 minutes.

For the cod. Add the whole cod loins to the curry sauce and simmer for 8–10 minutes or until cooked through but still holding their shape.

To serve. Remove the cod loins and place one on each serving plate. Finish the sauce by adding the double cream, fresh tomatoes, chopped coriander and lime juice. Spoon the sauce over the cod loins and serve with the hot rice and bread.

FILLET OF SALMON WITH BUTTER BEAN AND SAFFRON STEW, IBÉRICO HAM AND CHARRED COURGETTE SERVES 4

The competition really started warming up when we were challenged to cook a two-course menu in 45 minutes for three previous *MasterChef* winners: James Nathan, Shelina Permalloo and Steven Wallis. I created this Mediterranean-inspired dish for the main course. While I was developing the recipe I had my parents taste it, and they gave it the 'thumbs up'. So after some fine-tuning I decided it was the right dish to impress. Luckily for me, it did!

For the bean stew
2 slices Ibérico ham, cut 5mm thick
olive oil
1 large Spanish onion, finely chopped
½ red pepper and ½ green pepper, diced
3 garlic cloves, finely chopped
125ml white wine
4 tablespoons brandy
1 tablespoon tomato purée
2 x 400g cans butter beans in water, drained
grated zest of 1 lemon
juice of ½ lemon
20g picked thyme leaves, chopped
a pinch of saffron threads
about 500ml chicken stock

For the courgettes
4 thick courgettes
olive oil

For the salmon
4 pieces of salmon fillet from the thick end (skin on), about 200g each, trimmed and pin-boned
olive oil
1 lemon, ends trimmed
salt and pepper to taste

To garnish
50g basil leaves, cut into julienne
150g spinach
fine shreds of lemon zest
extra virgin olive oil

For the bean stew. Cut some of the lean Ibérico ham into 12 small batons and reserve for the garnish. Cut the remaining ham into 5mm dice. Heat a heavy, deep frying pan and gently fry the diced ham to render some of the fat. Add a splash of oil to the pan followed by the onion. Soften the onion for 5 minutes before adding the peppers and garlic. Sauté for 2–3 minutes. Add the white wine and boil until almost all evaporated, then add the brandy and set it alight to flambé; let the flames die down.

Next stir in the tomato purée and cook for 2–3 minutes. Add the beans to the pan along with the lemon zest and juice, thyme and saffron. Stir well. Pour in just enough stock to cover the ingredients. Bring to the boil, then reduce the heat and simmer gently for 10–15 minutes, adding more stock as needed so the beans are kept covered. Season with salt and pepper.

For the courgettes. While the stew is simmering, slice the ends off the courgettes and cut them across in half. 'Turn' each piece of courgette into a quenelle shape, keeping the skin on one side. (If you don't feel up to shaping quenelles you can just cut the courgettes across into thick discs.) Toss the courgettes in olive oil and season.

Heat a ridged griddle pan. Add the courgettes, skin side down first, and cook for 5–7 minutes on each side or until tender and charred. Be sure to leave the courgettes long enough without moving them to get neat charred lines on the vegetable. Add to the bean stew and keep hot.

For the salmon. Preheat the oven to 200°C/Gas Mark 6. Heat a large ovenproof frying pan. Season the skin on the fillets and slash it across at 2.5cm intervals. Rub the skin with oil, then place the fillets skin side down in the hot pan and cook for 5–6 minutes or until the skin is crisp. Meanwhile, cut the lemon into four 1cm-thick discs. Place these in the pan alongside the salmon so they can caramelise. When the skin is crisp, flip the fillets over and transfer the pan to the oven to finish cooking for 3 minutes.

To serve. Add most of the basil and the spinach to the bean stew, then taste and season as needed. Ladle a mound of bean stew into each large white bowl, adding two 'turned' courgettes, and sit the salmon alongside with a caramelised slice of lemon beside it. Garnish with the reserved batons of Ibérico ham, shreds of lemon zest and the remaining julienne of basil and dress with some extra virgin olive oil.

CURED MACKEREL, SMOKED MACKEREL PÂTÉ, CUCUMBER, PICKLED MUSHROOMS,
POMEGRANATE VINAIGRETTE SERVES 4

FROM THE SERIES

I'm a competitive person – in every part of my life – and I don't like to lose. After the round of the competition when I was literally knocked down a peg or two by Marcus Wareing, I knew I had to find something deep within myself to drag me back into the running for the three. This was my 'comeback' dish. I deliberated, practised, tasted, practised more and finally perfected it. The judges knew two things about me then – that I was as good as they had thought I was and, more importantly, that I wanted it so much and wasn't prepared to go down without a fight!

For the baguettes
500ml lukewarm water
1 tablespoon dried yeast
1 tablespoon caster sugar
660g strong white bread flour
2 teaspoons salt
1 tablespoon vegetable oil
beaten egg, for glazing

For the cured mackerel
a small bunch of dill
50g grated fresh horseradish
150g salt
300g caster sugar
4 mackerel fillets (skin on), pin-boned
olive oil, for frying
25g unsalted butter

For the smoked mackerel pâté
2 skinless mackerel fillets
50g salt
50g caster sugar
alder smoking chips
a squeeze of lemon juice
75g cream cheese
40g Greek-style yoghurt

For the pickled mushrooms
150g small cremini or portabellini mushrooms
100ml cider vinegar
75ml white wine vinegar
100g caster sugar
1 star anise
1 cinnamon stick
3 cloves
1 teaspoon yellow mustard seeds

For the pickled cucumber
1 large cucumber
3 tablespoons red wine vinegar
3 shakes of Tabasco sauce
2 tablespoons caster sugar

For the pomegranate vinaigrette
seeds and juice from 1 pomegranate
1 tablespoon honey
1 tablespoon red wine vinegar
75ml olive oil
salt and pepper to taste

To garnish
baby salad leaves
red amaranth

For the baguettes. Pour the water into a large mixing bowl and sprinkle the yeast on top followed by the sugar. Cover with a tea towel and leave until bubbling. Put the flour, salt and oil in another large mixing bowl and make a well in the centre. Pour the bubbling yeast mixture into the well and mix with the flour to make a dough that pulls away from the sides of the bowl. Turn out on to a lightly floured surface and knead for about 10 minutes or until smooth and elastic. Shape the dough into a ball and place in an oiled bowl. Cover with clingfilm and leave to rise in a warm place for 1–2 hours or until doubled in size.

Turn out the dough on to a lightly floured work surface. Knock back the dough and fold it into itself several times, then divide into two equal pieces. Stretch each piece into an oblong, then fold into itself from each long side and roll into a baguette shape. The top should be smooth with a seam running down the base. Line a large baking tray with baking parchment and dust lightly with flour. Place the baguettes on the tray, leaving at least 12.5cm between them. Leave to rise for about 1 hour or until doubled in size.

Preheat the oven to 220°C/Gas Mark 7 and put an empty roasting tin in the bottom of the oven. Slash the top of each baguette with a sharp knife and brush with beaten egg. Working quickly, place the tray of baguettes in the oven, then add about a litre of cold water to the empty roasting tin and close the oven door as fast as possible to keep in the steam created. Bake the baguettes for 30 minutes or until golden brown and they sound hollow when tapped on the base. Cool on a wire rack.

For the cured mackerel. Combine the dill, horseradish, salt and sugar in a small food processor and blitz until smooth. Trim the mackerel fillets so they are all the same size. Place them side by side in

continued on page 176

continued from page 175

a deep dish and cover with the dill cure. Cover with clingfilm and leave in the fridge for at least 2 hours. Remove the fish from the cure and rinse under cold water. Keep in the fridge until needed.

For the smoked mackerel pâté.
Lay the mackerel fillets on a plate. Mix together the salt and sugar and sprinkle over the fillets. Set aside for 30 minutes, then rinse with cold water and pat dry with kitchen paper.

Set up a stovetop smoker on the hob, add the chips and heat. When they are smoking add the fillets and smoke for 10–15 minutes or until nearly cooked but retaining a slight pink colour. Flake the fish into a blender and add the lemon juice, cream cheese and yoghurt. Season with salt and pepper. Pulse the mixture to a coarse pâté. Transfer to a clean bowl and keep in the fridge until needed.

For the pickled mushrooms. Cut larger mushrooms in half or into slices; leave small ones whole. Warm through the remaining ingredients in a small saucepan over a low heat until the sugar has dissolved. Bring to the boil, then remove from the heat. Add the mushrooms to the pan and set aside to pickle.

For the pickled cucumber. Using a vegetable peeler, shave off lengths from the cucumber, from one end to the other; stop when you reach the seeds and shave lengths from the other side. Discard the lengths that are mainly skin. You want 16 very thin cucumber slices with skin at the edges.

Heat together the red wine vinegar, Tabasco, sugar and some seasoning until the sugar has dissolved. Allow to cool a little, then add eight of the cucumber slices and set aside to pickle for no more than an hour. (Reserve the remaining eight slices to chargrill.)

For the chargrilled cucumber. Heat a ridged griddle pan over a medium heat. Chargrill the reserved cucumber slices until golden brown on each side and marked with charred lines. Remove and set aside.

To chargrill the baguettes. Cut 16 thin slices from the baguettes and chargrill them on both sides. Reserve.

For the pomegranate vinaigrette. Warm the pomegranate seeds and juice in a small saucepan. Remove from the heat, add the honey and red wine vinegar and stir well. Leave to infuse for 10 minutes before adding the olive oil. Season with salt and pepper. Set aside.

To finish the cured mackerel. Heat a frying pan until hot, then add the olive oil and the cured mackerel fillets, skin side down. Fry for 3–4 minutes or until the skin is golden and crisp. Add the butter to the pan, then turn the fillets over. Cook for a further 2 minutes, spooning the foaming butter over the fillets. Remove from the heat.

To serve. Lay two slices of chargrilled cucumber lengthways on each plate. Wrap a spoonful of pâté in a drained slice of pickled cucumber and sit that on one end of the chargrilled slices. Place a cured mackerel fillet in the centre. Wrap some salad leaves in a second drained pickled cucumber slice and place at the other end of the chargrilled slices. Garnish the plate with pickled mushrooms, pomegranate vinaigrette and red amaranth, and serve with the chargrilled slices of baguette.

RED MULLET BALLOTINE WITH CHORIZO, OLIVE, TOMATO AND TAPENADE SERVES 4

Once I had reached the *MasterChef* Final, it's fair to say I was losing my mind! Trying to think of three plates of food that stood between me and *being crowned the winner* was a pretty harrowing experience. The first time I made this dish, it bombed! Mum and I spent about 12 hours in the kitchen one Saturday designing the dish, only for the first 'take' to be a car-crash. We finished at midnight, she and Dad went home, and I went to bed feeling completely exhausted and dejected about my chances. Lucky for me she knocked on my front door at 7am the next morning and wasn't taking no for an answer! We were in and out of the supermarkets by 8am and cooking again an hour later! After some serious redesigning and tasting, the dish was how I wanted it. This was the first course of what would become my Final menu.

2 x 500g red mullets
olive oil, for frying
lemon juice

For the red mullet farce
50g skinned chorizo, finely chopped
2 x 300g red mullets, filleted, skinned and chopped
15g pitted black olives
15g dried breadcrumbs
a few sprigs of coriander
1 egg yolk

For the spicy ketchup
500g vine-ripened tomatoes
75g caster sugar
2 teaspoons sea salt
1 teaspoon white peppercorns
olive oil, for drizzling
3 garlic cloves, sliced
a small bunch of basil
500ml tomato juice
dash of Tabasco sauce

For the confit tomatoes
250g Piccolini tomatoes
olive oil, for drizzling

For the spicy peppers
1 tablespoon olive oil
1 small red onion, diced
50g raw cooking chorizo
½ teaspoon ras el hanout
215g roasted red peppers from a jar (drained weight), cut into strips
5 pitted black olives, halved
a small handful of coriander sprigs, chopped

For the tapenade
100g pitted black olives
20g drained anchovy fillets in oil
10g capers, rinsed and drained
½ garlic clove, peeled
1½ teaspoons olive oil
salt and pepper to taste

To serve
4 slices of toasted bread
4 long slices of cured chorizo, fried
basil cress, to garnish
olive oil, for drizzling

For the red mullets. Scale and clean the fish, reserving the livers for the farce. Butterfly the whole red mullets by removing the backbone and all other bones, leaving the two fillets of each fish still attached with their skin.

For the red mullet farce. Heat a small frying pan and fry the chorizo over a high heat until golden (you won't need to add any oil as the chorizo will be oily enough). Drain on kitchen paper and set aside.

Put the remaining farce ingredients, including the reserved mullet livers, in a food processor and pulse to a coarse texture. Mix in the chorizo and pulse for a few more seconds. Tightly roll the mixture in clingfilm, shaping into a sausage about 2.5cm in diameter. Place in the fridge to firm up.

For the spicy ketchup. Preheat the oven to 180°C/Gas Mark 4. Put the tomatoes in an ovenproof dish and sprinkle with the sugar, salt, peppercorns and a drizzle of olive oil. Roast for 1 hour, stirring every 20 minutes. Add the garlic, basil and tomato juice and stir to mix, then roast for a further 30 minutes. Tip the mixture into a food processor and blitz until smooth. (Leave the oven on, reduced to 100°C/Gas Mark ½, for the confit tomatoes.) Pass through a sieve into a clean saucepan and boil to reduce by a third. Add the Tabasco and seasoning to taste. Set aside, ready to reheat for serving.

For the ballotines. Unwrap the farce and cut it across into two pieces. Place a piece of farce in the centre of each butterflied mullet (on the skin where the backbone was) and wrap the fish over and around the farce to completely enclose it. Wrap each ballotine tightly in clingfilm, then wrap in a second layer of clingfilm. Place in the freezer to firm up for 1 hour. (Meanwhile, make the confit tomatoes, spicy peppers and tapenade.)

For the confit tomatoes. Blanch the tomatoes in a pan of boiling water for 1 minute, then refresh in iced water and remove the skins. Place on a baking tray, drizzle with olive oil and season with salt. Cook in the oven for 1 hour.

For the spicy peppers. Heat the olive oil in a saucepan and sauté the onion and chorizo with the ras el hanout for 3–4 minutes or until the onion is softened. Add the peppers and cook for a further 3 minutes. Stir in the olives, coriander and 1 tablespoon of the spicy ketchup. Set aside, ready to reheat for serving.

For the tapenade. Combine all the ingredients in a food processor and blitz to a coarse purée. Set aside.

To finish the ballotines. Remove from the freezer and cut each across (still wrapped in clingfilm) in half. Trim each piece into a 5cm disc. Now remove the clingfilm and season the discs on both sides. Heat an ovenproof frying pan until hot, then add some olive oil and pan-fry the discs for 1 minute on each flat side. Transfer the pan to the oven, increasing the temperature to 180°C/Gas Mark 4, to finish cooking for 5–6 minutes. Remove from the oven and season with a squeeze of lemon juice.

To serve. For each serving, place a metal chef's/presentation ring that is larger in diameter than your ballotine discs in the centre of the plate. Spoon in a layer of spicy ketchup followed by spoonfuls of spicy peppers; lift off the ring. Top with a disc of ballotine. Arrange some confit tomatoes around the edge. Spread the toast with tapenade and place a fried chorizo slice on top. Place the toast on the plate, leaning on the ballotine. Garnish with basil cress and drizzles of olive oil.

Making Red Mullet Ballotine with Chorizo, Olive, Tomato and Tapenade (see page 178).

CRAB RISOTTO, PARMESAN SNAP SERVES 4

FROM THE SERIES

When Larkin, Nat and I found out we were going to Italy we were all buzzing. We had just found out we were in the final three; we were now flying to Italy to learn from some of the world's best chefs in the country's finest restaurants. If I could eat only one country's cuisine for the rest of my life it would be Italian food, so for me the experience was a dream come true – learning to cook the food I loved from the people who knew it best. I soon learned that Italians never mix fish with cheese (oops!), but even though it's not traditional, the Italian artists who tried this dish loved my Parmesan crisps stuffed with white crab meat and zingy lemon and herbs.

---

4 cooked brown crabs, about 500g each
micro cress, to garnish

For the crab stock
1–2 tablespoons olive oil
2 white onions, quartered
6 garlic cloves, lightly crushed
4 celery sticks and 2 carrots, chopped
1 bulb of fennel, chopped
10 mushrooms, roughly chopped
2 tablespoons tomato purée
500ml white wine
4 bay leaves
stalks from a small bunch of parsley,
    finely chopped
2 tablespoons black peppercorns

For the lemon oil
50ml each of olive oil and vegetable oil
2 bay leaves
grated zest of 1 lemon
juice of ¹/₂ lemon
4 black peppercorns

For the Parmesan crisps
100g Parmesan, freshly grated
a pinch of cayenne pepper
juice of 1 lemon

For the risotto
1–2 tablespoons olive oil
4 spring onions, finely sliced
grated zest and juice of 2 lemons
3 garlic cloves, finely chopped
2 medium red chillies, deseeded and
    finely chopped
250g Arborio risotto rice
300ml white wine
about 50g crème fraîche
125g Parmesan, freshly grated
leaves from a small bunch of coriander,
    chopped
salt and white pepper

For the crab. Remove the meat from the crabs, keeping the white and brown meat separate; set aside. Break up the crab shells a little using a hammer or rolling pin.

For the crab stock. Heat the olive oil in a large pan and sauté the vegetables until soft. Add the shells from the crabs and sauté for 5 minutes. Stir in the tomato purée and cook for 2 minutes, then add the wine, herbs and peppercorns. Bring to the boil and simmer for a few minutes. Pour in 2 litres of cold water to cover everything. Bring back to the boil, then leave to simmer for 1–1¹/₂ hours. (While the stock is simmering, make the lemon oil and Parmesan crisps.)

When the stock is ready, skim off any scum from the surface, then pass through a fine sieve lined with muslin into a clean pan, pressing the shells and vegetables in the sieve with a ladle to remove all of the flavourful liquid. Keep the stock warm on a low simmer.

For the lemon oil. Gently heat the two oils in a small saucepan until just warm – you should be able to touch the oil with your finger. Remove from the heat and add the other ingredients. Cover and leave to infuse for at least 1 hour. Strain the oil and reserve in a squeezy bottle for dressing the risotto.

For the Parmesan crisps. Preheat the oven to 160°C/Gas Mark 3 and line a baking tray with greaseproof paper. Set four 8cm metal chef's/presentation rings on the lined tray. Spoon enough Parmesan into each mould to make a thin layer at the bottom. Bake for about 10 minutes or until bubbling. Remove

and allow to cool slightly, then lift off the moulds and shape each Parmesan crisp by laying it over a rolling pin. Leave to set.

Just before serving, mix the white crabmeat with the cayenne, lemon juice and salt and pepper to taste. Fill the crisps with this mixture.

For the risotto. Heat the olive oil in a large sauté pan and gently cook the spring onions with the lemon zest, garlic and chillies until soft. Add the rice and stir to coat well. Add the white wine to the simmering crab stock, then ladle a third of the stock over the rice. Cook, stirring, until the stock has been absorbed. Continue ladling in the stock, letting each addition be absorbed before adding the next, and stirring constantly. The cooking of the risotto will take about 20 minutes and the rice should be al dente at the end. Adjust the seasoning with lemon juice, salt and white pepper. Remove from the heat.

Mix the brown crab meat with an equal amount of crème fraîche and stir this into the risotto along with the Parmesan and chopped coriander.

To serve. Spoon the risotto into bowls, dress with lemon oil and garnish with micro cress. Serve topped with a Parmesan crisp.

LITTLE J'S CHILLI CRAB NOODLES

SERVES 4

My mum, Jacky, is known in the family as 'Little J'. I have her to thank for my being an adventurous cook – she encouraged us to eat experimentally from a young age. I love to try new flavours and there aren't any foods that scare me off. I like spicy food and, in particular, chilli. I grow Thai red chillies at home on the windowsill. You can dry them and then blitz in a spice mill to make your own chilli flakes. There's no neat and tidy way to eat this: you have to just grab the crab claws and pick out every last morsel of sweet white crab meat, although you can use chopsticks to eat the noodles if you prefer.

250g dried fine egg noodles
4 tablespoons groundnut oil
6 large garlic cloves, finely chopped
3 medium red chillies, finely chopped
3 tablespoons grated fresh ginger
8–12 brown crab claws (or more, depending on size), gently cracked on one side with a rolling pin
1 tablespoon fresh lime juice
4 spring onions, finely chopped
micro coriander or chopped coriander, to garnish

For the chilli sauce
5 tablespoons tomato ketchup
1 tablespoon sweet chilli sauce
2 tablespoons light soy sauce
1 tablespoon caster sugar
2 teaspoons cornflour
salt and pepper to taste

For the chilli sauce. Combine the ingredients for the chilli sauce with 250ml water, whisking well. Set aside.

For the noodles. Cook the egg noodles following the packet instructions. Drain and set aside.

For the crab. Heat the groundnut oil in a large wok, add the garlic, chillies and ginger, and stir-fry for 30 seconds. Add the crab claws and cook for 2–3 minutes, shaking the wok and tossing the ingredients together. Stir the chilli sauce, then add it to the wok and stir-fry for a further minute. Add the lime juice and 150ml water. The sauce will be very loose but after a few minutes the cornflour will start to thicken it. When the sauce begins to thicken, add the cooked noodles and mix well with the sauce and crab. Cook for 2 more minutes.

To serve. Divide the crab and noodles among four bowls and garnish with the spring onions and coriander.

There's no neat way to eat this - just dive in!

SAFFRON CLAMS MARINIÈRE, MINI BAGUETTE

SERVES 4

Shellfish cooked simply and eaten with your fingers is the kind of food that excites me! I love simple food done well, with minimal fuss and maximum flavour. Seafood is one of the best ways to achieve this. Cook the shellfish quickly, throw in some wine, garlic, chilli and fresh herbs and you can't go far wrong. You can try this dish with mussels, cockles or even prawns and langoustines. Just allow a few extra minutes for the prawns or langoustines to cook through.

For the baguettes
250g white bread flour
5g salt
1 x 7g sachet fast-action dried yeast
3 tablespoons olive oil
170ml lukewarm water

For the clams
4 dozen littleneck clams, well scrubbed
3 tablespoons olive oil
4 garlic cloves, finely chopped
2 shallots, finely diced
300ml dry white wine
a pinch of saffron threads
150g unsalted butter, cut into pieces
juice of 1 lemon
a small bunch of chives, finely chopped
sea salt and white pepper to taste
2 tablespoons finely chopped flat-leaf
    parsley

For the mini baguettes. Put the flour, salt and yeast into a free-standing electric mixer fitted with a dough hook. Start mixing on a slow speed while gradually adding the oil and then the lukewarm water. When fully incorporated, continue mixing for 5 minutes. Turn the speed up to medium and mix/knead for 10 minutes to create a shiny elastic dough. (Alternatively you can mix and knead the dough by hand.) Tip the ball of dough into a lightly oiled bowl, cover with a wet tea towel and leave to rise in a warm place for at least 2 hours or until doubled in size.

Turn out the dough on to a lightly floured work surface. Knock back the dough to deflate it, then divide into four equal pieces. Stretch each piece into an oblong, then fold into itself from each long side and roll into a baguette shape. The top should be smooth with a seam running down the bottom. Line a large baking tray with baking parchment and dust lightly with flour. Place the baguettes on the tray, leaving at least 12.5cm between them. Leave to rise for about 1 hour or until doubled in size.

Preheat the oven to 200°C/Gas Mark 6 and put an empty roasting tray in the bottom of the oven. Slash the top of each baguette with a sharp knife. Working quickly, place the tray of baguettes in the oven, then add about a litre of water to the empty roasting tray and close the oven door as fast as possible to keep in the steam created. Bake the baguettes for 20 minutes, then reduce the heat to 180°C/Gas Mark 4 and bake for a further 5 minutes. Cool on a wire rack.

For the clams. To clean the clams, immerse them in a deep bowl of clean cold water and leave for at least an hour: they will purge themselves of any grit. Lift them out of the water into a clean bowl and add some ice. Set aside until ready to use.

Heat the olive oil in a large non-reactive saucepan with a lid. Add the garlic and shallots and sweat until translucent. Add the wine and saffron followed by the clams. Cover and steam, shaking the pan occasionally, for 5–7 minutes or until the clams open. Take out the clams with a slotted spoon (keep the pan on the heat) and put them into a clean serving bowl; discard any clams that have not opened. Whisk the butter into the sauce before seasoning with the lemon juice, a pinch of salt and some white pepper. Add the chives and chopped parsley, then pour the sauce over the clams.

To serve. Spoon the clams into four pots or bowls and serve with the mini baguettes for soaking up the juices.

Minimal fuss and maximum flavour.

BUTTERNUT SQUASH SOUP, ROASTED TOMATO FOCACCIA SERVES 4

It amazes me when I hear soup labelled as 'old-fashioned' or 'an easy starter'. When I'm entertaining guests, I want the food to be good, probably even great, but know that my guests haven't come just to eat. A well-made soup can be prepared in advance, and will give you time to chat to your guests over some canapés before reheating the soup just before serving. A few fancy additions can transform even the humblest soup, and making your own bread will surely create the 'wow factor'.

For the focaccia bread
500g white bread flour
1 heaped tablespoon coarse semolina
2 x 7g sachets fast-action dried yeast
320ml lukewarm water
50ml olive oil
150g sunblush tomatoes, drained
75g walnut pieces
12 small sprigs of thyme
extra virgin olive oil, for drizzling

For the soup
1 large butternut squash, cut lengthways in half
olive oil
1 small red chilli
1 banana shallot, finely diced
1 garlic clove, finely chopped
2 tablespoons chopped lemon thyme
500ml vegetable stock
4 tablespoons plain yoghurt

For the caramelised onion
1 red onion, finely sliced
a knob of butter
1 tablespoon brown sugar
2 tablespoons red wine vinegar
a sprig of thyme
salt and black and white pepper

To garnish
plain yoghurt
Greek basil leaves
extra virgin olive oil

For the focaccia. Mix together the flour, semolina, yeast and a pinch of salt in a large bowl. Mix the warm water with the olive oil. Make a well in the flour mixture, then gradually add the liquid – mix initially with a fork and then with your hands to make a ball of dough. Turn out on to a floured surface and knead for 10 minutes or until smooth and elastic. Place in a clean oiled bowl, cover with clingfilm and set aside to rise for about 1 hour or until doubled in size.

Preheat the oven to 200°C/Gas Mark 6. Line a 26 x 32cm shallow baking tray with greaseproof paper. Knock back the dough to deflate it, then turn out on to the tray. Prod the dough out to the sides and into the corners to make an even layer. Sprinkle with salt, then press the tomatoes and walnuts into the dough, along with the thyme. Drizzle with extra virgin olive oil. Bake for 30 minutes or until cooked through (the bread will sound hollow when tapped on the base). Cool on a wire rack to serve warm.

For the squash. Place the squash halves skin side down in a roasting tray. Season the flesh with salt and pepper and drizzle with olive oil. Put the red chilli in a bowl and dress it with a little olive oil before adding to the roasting tray. Roast for 30–40 minutes or until the squash is

soft. Meanwhile, add the diced shallot and garlic to 1 tablespoon of olive oil in a heated frying pan and cook gently until soft and translucent; set aside.

For the caramelised onion. While the squash is in the oven, cook the red onion with the butter, brown sugar, vinegar and thyme in a pan over a gentle heat for 30 minutes, stirring occasionally.

For the soup. Remove the squash from the oven and allow to cool slightly, then scoop the flesh from the skin and add to the shallot and garlic mixture in the frying pan. Finely slice the chilli, discarding the seeds, and add to the pan along with the chopped lemon thyme. Fry the mixture, stirring well, for 4–5 minutes to intensify the flavour. Transfer to a food processor, add the stock and blitz to a smooth consistency. Season with some salt and white pepper, then taste and add more if needed. Add the yoghurt and 1 tablespoon olive oil. Blend the soup again until completely smooth. Pour into a saucepan and reheat gently.

To serve. Spoon some of the caramelised red onion into each soup bowl. Ladle the soup over and dress with yoghurt, extra virgin olive oil and torn basil. Accompany with large portions of focaccia.

CHORIZO AND ANCHOVY PAPPARDELLE SERVES 4

When it comes to midweek cooking, it's easy to become lazy, particularly after a long day at work. By keeping a selection of ingredients in the fridge and storecupboard I always know I'm only a few fresh tomatoes or prawns or an oozy block of Brie away from a tasty meal in minutes. With this in mind, dried pasta, cooking chorizo, anchovies, garlic, lemon, vinegars and oils are always in plentiful supply at home. I absolutely adore pasta. I could live on it quite easily, and the options are endless when it comes to being creative. This is my take on an anchovy and chorizo pappardelle with some serious attitude.

400g dried pappardelle
extra virgin olive oil, for drizzling

For the sauce
1 tablespoon olive oil
400g cooking chorizo, sliced into
    5mm discs
250g vine-ripened tomatoes, roughly
    diced
1 teaspoon dried chilli flakes
2 tablespoons dried oregano
2 garlic cloves, finely chopped
20 fresh marinated anchovy fillets, drained
salt and pepper to taste
200g pitted black olives, halved
4 tablespoons chopped parsley
juice of 1/2 lemon
extra virgin olive oil

For the pasta. Bring a large pan of salted water to the boil. Add the pasta and cook according to the packet instructions, until al dente.

For the sauce. While the pasta is cooking, set a wide high-sided frying pan over a medium heat and heat the olive oil. Add the chorizo and gently fry for 2–3 minutes to release the colourful oil and aroma, turning the chorizo halfway through. Add the tomatoes, chilli flakes, oregano, garlic and anchovies to the pan and cook for a further 3–4 minutes or until softened. Season with salt and pepper before adding the black olives and, finally, the parsley.

Using tongs, lift the cooked spaghetti from its pan of water and into the sauce (or drain the pasta in a colander, then tip into the sauce). Combine the spaghetti with the sauce and add the lemon juice.

To serve. Divide among four bowls and dress each with a drizzle of extra virgin olive oil.

A great meal in minutes.

PAN-ROASTED CHICKEN AND BUBBLING GOAT'S CHEESE WITH BALSAMIC TOMATOES AND A COURGETTE SALAD

SERVES 4

If *MasterChef* taught me one thing, it is the art of matching flavours. It is that process of deciding if something is there out of necessity, or is a frivolity – does it 'add' something to the dish? It is about how flavours are layered to complement one another. Before entering the competition I was often guilty of over-complicating a dish. The one here is stripped back to basics, an example of taking a humble set of everyday ingredients and matching them to make a wonderfully flavourful dish, using everyday kitchen equipment.

4 courgettes, ends removed, sliced
   lengthways
25g basil leaves
1 red chilli, sliced
olive oil
juice of 1 lemon
salt and pepper to taste
4 boneless chicken breasts (skin on)
50g unsalted butter
4 large vine-ripened tomatoes, cut in half
4 tablespoons balsamic vinegar
a few sprigs of thyme
4 discs of goat's cheese, about 1cm thick
100g cooking chorizo, sliced
extra virgin olive oil, to finish

For the courgettes. Put the courgettes, half the basil leaves, the chilli and 2 tablespoons olive oil into a mixing bowl and turn with your hands until the courgettes are coated with the flavoured oil. Heat a ridged griddle pan to smoking point over a high heat. Add the courgette slices, four or five at a time, laying them out flat. Sear on each side for 3 minutes or until softened and marked with charred lines. When all the courgette slices have been seared, put them back in the bowl. Dress with the lemon juice and salt and pepper to taste, then cover the bowl with clingfilm to keep warm. Set aside.

For the chicken. Preheat the oven to 200°C/Gas Mark 6. Set an ovenproof frying pan on a medium heat and add a glug of olive oil. Season the chicken breasts on the skin side before placing them, skin side down, in the hot pan. Leave to cook for 5–6 minutes to crisp the skin (don't be tempted to move the chicken), then add the butter. When it has melted, spoon it over the chicken and cook for 2 more minutes, basting with the foaming butter. Season the breasts, then turn them over. Place the pan in the oven to finish cooking, which will take 5–6 minutes. Remove from the oven and leave to rest for 3–4 minutes.

For the balsamic tomatoes. Once you have put the chicken into the oven, you can prepare the remaining ingredients. Heat the grill to medium (for the cheese). Heat a frying pan and add 1 tablespoon of olive oil. Season the tomatoes, then put them, cut side down, in the pan and cook for 5–6 minutes or until lightly caramelised. Add the balsamic vinegar and continue to cook for 1 minute. Turn the tomatoes over and cook for a further 2 minutes. Remove from the heat and keep warm.

For the goat's cheese. Pick the leaves from the thyme and press them gently into each goat's cheese disc. Lightly season with salt and add a drizzle of olive oil. Arrange on a baking tray and grill for 5–6 minutes or until bubbling and warmed through.

For the chorizo. Meanwhile, heat a small frying pan and gently fry the chorizo until caramelised and cooked through. Add the chorizo and the rest of the basil leaves, roughly torn, to the courgettes and mix together gently.

To serve. Mound the courgette and chorizo salad in the centre of each plate. Slice the chicken breasts on the diagonal and arrange skin side up on the salad. Place two balsamic tomato halves alongside and rest the bubbling goat's cheese on top. Finish with a drizzle of extra virgin olive oil.

CHICKEN BURGER, SCRATCHINGS AND LOLLIPOPS WITH COLESLAW, FRIES AND BARBECUE SAUCE SERVES 4

When I made a chicken burger on *MasterChef* there were only seven contestants left, each vying for a place as a Semi-Finalist, and the majority of us hadn't seen how the others cooked. As we were all talking backstage, I mentioned that I would be making a chicken burger, which was met with astonishment (up to this point my food had been classic and refined). I wanted to show something different: it was the risk-taker in me coming out to play. Calculated risks can sometimes pay off in spectacular fashion! My chicken burger was so popular that it booked me my Semi-Final place and was on the menu in the *MasterChef* restaurant at the BBC Good Food Show this summer.

4 large, firm Maris Piper potatoes
oil for deep-frying
8 rashers streaky bacon
4 artisan white rolls, split open
2 ripe beef tomatoes, sliced
8 crisp lettuce leaves
4 large pickled gherkins, sliced

For the chicken burgers
4 boneless corn-fed chicken breasts (skin on)
4 garlic cloves, crushed
picked leaves from 2 sprigs of soft lemon thyme, finely chopped
200g seasoned flour
3 eggs, beaten
200g panko breadcrumbs
sunflower oil, for frying

For the lollipops
8 chicken drumsticks (skin on)
1 teaspoon each onion salt, garlic granules, celery salt, white pepper, ground ginger, paprika, dried marjoram, dried parsley, dried sage and dried oregano
100g super-fine natural breadcrumbs
100g seasoned flour
2 eggs, beaten

For the mayonnaise
2 egg yolks
1 teaspoon Dijon mustard
1 tablespoon white wine vinegar
250ml sunflower oil
1 teaspoon lemon juice
1 tablespoon each finely chopped parsley, soft lemon thyme, tarragon, chives, oregano and basil

For the coleslaw
1 large carrot
1 small white cabbage
1 large white onion
1 red onion

For the barbecue sauce
4 tablespoons tomato ketchup
4 tablespoons brown sauce
2 teaspoons dark soy sauce
2 teaspoons Worcestershire sauce
2 teaspoons malt vinegar
1 teaspoon English mustard powder
2 tablespoons clear honey
1 tablespoon golden caster sugar
salt and black and white pepper to taste

For the chicken burgers. Remove the skin from each breast, being careful to keep the skin in a single piece; reserve the skin for the scratchings. Cut each skinned breast into three pieces, then put in a food processor and pulse until coarsely ground. Add the garlic, thyme and some salt and pepper and mix well. Mould into four burgers about 2.5cm thick. Firm up in the fridge for about 1 hour.

Dredge the burgers with seasoned flour, then dip in the beaten eggs and, finally, coat with breadcrumbs. Keep in the fridge until needed.

For the lollipops. Take one chicken drumstick and carefully cut around the skin, down to the bone, at the thin, knuckle end. Holding the thick, meaty end, stand the drumstick on its knuckle and cut down the lower part of the bone to remove the knuckle and any cartilage. Using a meat cleaver, cut the exposed bone down to a neat diagonal 'lollipop' stick.

Gently work a small knife inside around the bone at the thick end, cutting the meat away from the bone, but keeping the meat in one piece. Work down the bone until you can remove the cylinder

of leg meat. Again stand the bone vertical and clean off any cartilage. Place the leg meat back on to the bone. Prepare the other drumsticks in the same way. Season the 'lollipops', then wrap individually in clingfilm, being sure each end is tightly wrapped and shaping the leg into a neat bauble shape. Tie each end with an extra piece of clingfilm.

Set a steamer over a deep pan of boiling water. Place the lollipops in the steamer and steam for 30 minutes. Remove from the steamer, unwrap the clingfilm and place on a plate. Chill the lollipops for 30 minutes.

Combine all of the dry seasonings and herbs with the breadcrumbs in a shallow bowl. Put the flour and beaten eggs in separate shallow bowls. Dredge the lollipops in flour, then dip into the eggs and, finally, coat with the herb crumbs. Keep in the fridge until needed.

For the fries. Peel the potatoes and cut into neat chips, then put them into a bowl of cold water and set aside for an hour.

For the scratchings. Preheat the oven to 220°C/Gas Mark 7. Lay the pieces of chicken skin flat on a baking sheet lined with greaseproof paper. Cover with a second baking sheet. Place in the oven to cook for 40 minutes or until crisp and golden. (Meanwhile, make the mayonnaise, coleslaw and barbecue sauce.)

For the mayonnaise. Put the egg yolks in a food processor with the mustard and vinegar. Blitz briefly to mix, then, with the machine running, very slowly

continued on page 196

continued from page 195

add the oil through the feed tube. When the mixture starts to emulsify and you see a slight colour change, you can add the oil more quickly, in a steady stream, but be careful not to pour too fast. Once the mayonnaise is thick and glossy, season with the lemon juice and salt and white pepper to taste. Add the herbs. Remove 2 tablespoons of the mayonnaise for the buns and keep in a small bowl in the fridge. Retain the rest for the coleslaw.

For the coleslaw. Finely shred all the vegetables. Put them in a bowl, add alf of the mayonnaise and mix well. Add more mayonnaise, to taste. Set aside in the fridge.

For the barbecue sauce. Combine all the ingredients in a small pan and whisk over a low heat until the sauce is just beginning to boil. Remove from the heat. Taste and adjust the seasoning. Add a few teaspoons of water if the sauce is too thick. Set aside.

To finish the burgers, fries and lollipops. Heat oil for deep-frying to 170°C. Drain the potatoes and rinse thoroughly. Dry with kitchen paper or a tea towel. Season well with salt, then lower into the hot oil and deep-fry for 10–12 minutes to cook the potatoes. Remove them from the oil. Increase the temperature of the oil to 190°C and deep-fry the potatoes for 6–7 minutes or until crisp and golden. Drain on kitchen paper and season with salt. Keep hot. Reduce the heat under the pan of oil so the temperature falls to 170°C again.

When you take the scratchings out of the oven, turn the temperature down to 180°C/Gas Mark 4. Fry the bacon in a heavy-based frying pan until crisp; remove and set aside. Pour enough sunflower oil into the frying pan to come halfway up your chicken burgers. Heat the oil, then fry the burgers for about 5 minutes on each side or until golden. Transfer to a baking tray and place in the oven to finish cooking for 12 minutes.

Meanwhile, heat a ridged griddle pan and toast the cut surfaces of the buns to give them charred lines. (Alternatively, toast under the grill.)

Once the pan of oil used for the fries has reached 170°C, deep-fry the lollipops for 5 minutes or until golden brown. Drain on kitchen paper and keep hot.

To serve. Spoon the reserved herb mayonnaise on to the bottom half of each bun. Place a chicken burger on top and add a tomato slice, two bacon rashers and two lettuce leaves. Put the top of the bun in place and pierce with a wooden skewer. Set a burger on each serving board or plate. Stand two lollipops next to the burger, leaning against each other upright. Put the fries into a tall pot lined with greaseproof paper, or directly on the board. Arrange the chicken scratchings in a neat pile on the board, leaning against the pot of fries if you like, and add the gherkins, plus barbecue sauce in a ramekin and coleslaw in a little pot or bowl.

Describe your first food memory…

There's one evening in particular, during a family holiday in a caravan in West Wales, my mum made a dish known as 'chicken with forty cloves of garlic'. The chicken is pot-roasted with the garlic, some stock, wine and herbs then served on a platter for all to see. That evening, six of us sat around a tiny round table in candlelight for hours – eating, laughing, talking and tearing at the juicy chicken with our fingers. It was magical.

Thoughts on your co-finalists?

Larkin and I hit it off straight away; we just clicked and I was so lucky to have someone that I had grown close to so quickly during the Finals of the competition. Some days were hard and you needed people around you that you could bounce off. Between us there is plenty of banter and we make each other laugh. I'm hoping to be collaborating with Larks in the near future. Nat is a bottle of pop! She's non-stop and can't help but be the centre of attention. She never fails to be noticed when she's in a room: that Cockney twang is instantly recognisable. She'll go on to be a great chef, I'm sure.

CHICKEN KIEV WITH A SUMMER SALAD SERVES 4

There is an awful lot to be said for the art of preparing a good chicken Kiev. Made well, with a little patience and love, these enticing creations can give every tastebud in your mouth a more-ish craving for another bite. Over the years I've eaten many, most of them lovingly prepared by my mum. Whenever chicken Kiev is on the menu over at her house it's normally at my youngest sister's request! You can prepare the chicken and most of the salad in advance, then cook just before serving.

For the chicken Kievs

200g soft unsalted butter

1 tablespoon each chopped tarragon, basil and parsley

2 garlic cloves, crushed and finely chopped to a paste

4 chicken supremes (skinless, boneless chicken breasts)

250g dried panko breadcrumbs

seasoned flour

4 egg yolks

300ml vegetable oil

For the salad

250g new potatoes (skin on)

16 fresh asparagus spears

1 cucumber

150g baby spinach leaves

75g sun-dried tomatoes

olive oil

1 thick slice day-old white bread, cut into 2.5cm dice

100g pancetta, cut into lardons

100g butter

For the vinaigrette

4 tablespoons olive oil

1 teaspoon Dijon mustard

1 teaspoon white wine vinegar

salt and white pepper to taste

For the Kievs. Mix together the soft butter, herbs and garlic and season with salt and pepper. Set aside. Remove the mini fillet from the underside of each supreme – it will easily pull away. Put the mini fillets between two sheets of clingfilm and pound until flattened to about 5mm thickness.

Place a supreme, skinned side up, on a chopping board and make a horizontal cut in the thickest part of the breast to fashion a small pocket. Take a generous teaspoonful of the butter mixture and put this into the pocket. Place a flattened mini fillet over the opening, to cover it completely, and smooth over the breast until it looks like a whole supreme again. Repeat to stuff the remaining supremes, then put them in the fridge to firm up.

Set out three shallow bowls on the worktop. Put the breadcrumbs in one bowl, the seasoned flour in another and the beaten egg yolks in the third. Dredge the supremes with flour, shaking off the excess, then dip in the yolks and, finally, coat with breadcrumbs. At this stage you can leave the Kievs in the fridge until needed.

For the salad. Drop the potatoes into a pan of boiling salted water and parboil for 10–15 minutes or until half cooked. Drain. Cut into halves or quarter if large, then set aside.

Snap off the tough ends of the asparagus spears, then peel the stalk thinly, from the base of the head to the end, using a vegetable peeler. Bring a pan of salted water to the boil and cook the asparagus spears for 3–4 minutes or until tender. Remove and immediately refresh in a bowl of iced water, then put the spears in a large salad bowl and set aside.

Remove the ends from the cucumber. Using a vegetable peeler shave off lengths from one end to the other

until you have 15–20 very thin cucumber ribbons. Add these to the asparagus, along with the spinach and sun-dried tomatoes. Cover and place in the fridge to keep fresh.

Set a frying pan over a medium heat and add 2–3 tablespoons olive oil to create a thin layer. Add the diced bread and fry until golden all over. Drain these croutons on kitchen paper. Set aside (keep in an airtight container if made ahead).

For the vinaigrette. Whisk the ingredients together in a small bowl. Set aside.

To finish the Kievs and salad. About half an hour before cooking, remove the Kievs from the fridge and bring them to room temperature. Preheat the oven to 200°C/Gas Mark 6. Heat the vegetable oil in a large, deep-sided frying pan to 190°C or until a cube of bread will turn golden in 30 seconds. Add the chicken Kievs to the hot oil and fry for 4–6 minutes on each side or until golden all over. Drain on kitchen paper, then place on a baking tray. Finish cooking in the oven, which will take about 15 minutes.

While the Kievs are in the oven, set a clean frying pan on a medium heat and add 1 tablespoon olive oil. Fry the pancetta lardons until golden; remove with a slotted spoon and set aside. Add another tablespoon of olive oil and then the new potatoes. Season with salt and pepper. Fry on a high heat until the potatoes start to turn golden brown. Add the butter and melt it, then continue cooking, basting the potatoes well with the buttery oil, until they are tender and golden. Remove and drain on kitchen paper.

To serve. Remove the salad from the fridge and dress lightly with the vinaigrette. Place the salad on the plates. Set a Kiev alongside and scatter the potatoes, lardons and croutons over the salad.

SPICED LAMB WITH MELTING BEANS AND GREEK SALAD SERVES 4

There are a few occasions each year when my dad manages to muscle in on Mum's kitchen. He's always there offering a strong pair of hands for any less desirable job, be it boning out poultry, filleting fish or just peeling spuds. But when it's Mum's birthday, Dad likes to take the reins so Mum can put her feet up. This year, he opted for a slow-cooked beef brisket with meltingly delicious, garlicky cannellini beans and a Greek salad. This is the dish we made that evening, but adapted to use the more widely available leg of lamb. The recipe can be easily multiplied to feed a crowd.

For the lamb
1 x 2.5kg leg of lamb
about 10 canned anchovies
2 garlic cloves, finely sliced
a few sprigs of rosemary
50g soft butter
2 teaspoons smoked paprika
1½ tablespoons ground cumin
salt and pepper to taste

For the beans
3 tablespoons olive oil
1 large white onion, finely diced
2 garlic cloves, lightly crushed
2 x 400g cans cannellini beans in water, drained
500ml chicken stock
1 tablespoon dried oregano
4 tablespoons chopped oregano

For the salad
a large handful of lamb's lettuce leaves
a large handful of rocket leaves
a large handful of baby spinach leaves
a handful of cherry tomatoes (ideally mixed colours), halved or quartered
½ cucumber, roughly chopped into 1cm dice
100g feta cheese, cut or broken into 1cm dice
juice of 1 lemon
extra virgin olive oil

For the lamb. Preheat the oven to 160°C/Gas Mark 3. With the tip of a knife make 2.5cm-deep incisions in the lamb all over the thickest part of the meat – about five on each side. Stuff an anchovy, a few slivers of garlic and a few rosemary tips into each slit. Mix the butter with the paprika, cumin and some salt and pepper. Using your hands, spread the mixture over the lamb, ensuring it is completely covered.

Set the lamb in a large roasting tray and pour 125ml of water around the lamb. Cover the tray tightly with foil and place in the oven to cook for 3 hours. Every hour, uncover the lamb and baste with the buttery juices in the tray, then cover again and return to the oven.

After 3 hours, remove the foil and turn the oven up to 200°C/Gas Mark 6. Roast for a further 30 minutes or until the crust on the lamb is golden brown and the meat is soft and falling from the bone. Remove from the oven and leave to rest for 30 minutes.

For the beans. While the lamb is resting, heat a deep saucepan, add the olive oil and gently fry the onion and garlic to soften; don't let them brown. Add the drained beans, then pour in enough stock to just cover the beans (you may not need all the stock). Add the dried oregano and a little seasoning. Bring to the boil, then simmer the beans for 10 minutes. Remove from the heat.

Ladle a quarter of the beans into a blender and pulse until smooth, then return them to the rest of the beans in the pan and stir well. The beans will now be creamy and slightly thickened. Check the seasoning before adding the fresh oregano. Keep hot.

For the salad. Prepare the salad by combining all the ingredients in a salad bowl, dressing with the lemon juice and a good drizzle of extra virgin olive oil.

To serve. Carve the lamb. Spoon the beans to the side of each plate and add a few slices of lamb, then serve with the salad.

Meltingly delicious.

LAMB'S LIVER, KIDNEY PUDDING, PEA, MUSHROOM AND RED WINE JUS SERVES 4

1 large, good-quality lamb's liver
  (lean, with minimal sinew)
2 tablespoons olive oil
25g unsalted butter
4 rashers streaky bacon
pea shoots, to garnish

For the suet pastry
50g self-raising flour
25g shredded beef suet
a pinch of salt

For the kidney pudding filling
2 lamb's kidneys, trimmed
1 tablespoon plain flour
1 teaspoon English mustard powder
100ml rich beef stock

For the pea purée
1½ teaspoons olive oil
20g unsalted butter
1 shallot, chopped
1 garlic clove, chopped
275g frozen peas
a small handful of mint, roughly chopped
250ml chicken stock

For the mushrooms
200g mixed wild mushrooms, cleaned
4 garlic cloves, peeled
1 tablespoon olive oil
50g cooked peeled chestnuts
25g unsalted butter
a small handful of flat-leaf parsley, chopped

For the red wine jus
250ml full-bodied good-quality red wine
250ml port
2 shallots, chopped
2 bay leaves
50g cold unsalted butter, cubed
a pinch of sugar
1 teaspoon redcurrant jelly
salt and black and white pepper to taste

For the suet pastry. Mix together the flour and suet with the salt and 3 tablespoons water in a small mixing bowl to make a dough. (Don't over-mix the dough: it should come together quite loosely.) Roll out thinly on a lightly floured surface. You will need four 50ml heatproof containers for the kidney puddings. Using a heatproof container as a guide, cut out four circles of suet pastry slightly bigger than the moulds plus four smaller circles to use as lids. Butter the heatproof containers and line with clingfilm, then line each with a round of pastry. Press in smoothly, taking care not to break the pastry. Set aside, with the pastry lids.

For the kidney puddings. Prepare the kidneys by cutting the lean meat away from the core. Season the flour with the mustard, salt and pepper and use to coat the kidneys. Fill the pastry-lined moulds with the kidneys and top up with stock. Place a pastry lid on top of each pudding and press down well to seal the edges.

Trim off any excess pastry. Cover each container with greaseproof paper and foil (make a fold in the centre of the paper and foil to allow for expansion), then place a rubber band around the container to hold the paper and foil in place.

Set the puddings in a steamer and steam for about 45 minutes. Remove and allow to cool slightly before gently removing the puddings from the moulds for serving. (Make the other elements of the dish while the puddings are steaming.)

For the pea purée. Heat the oil and butter in a saucepan and sweat the shallot and garlic until soft and translucent. Add the peas, mint and stock and leave to simmer gently for 10 minutes. Transfer to a blender and blend until smooth. Pass through a sieve into a jug. Season and check the consistency. If the purée is too thin, gently heat until simmering and slightly thickened; if it's too thick add a little more stock to loosen it. Transfer to a squeezy bottle and keep warm in a pan of water.

For the mushrooms. Cut large mushrooms in half and leave smaller mushrooms whole. Bring a small pan of water to the boil and blanch the garlic in a bowl of iced water. Repeat this process three times, using the same pan

continued on page 204

continued from page 203

of boiling water. Heat a large frying pan with the olive oil until really hot, then add the mushrooms and cook for 5 minutes, tossing them. Add the whole chestnuts and blanched garlic and sauté for a few more minutes. Add the butter and let it melt and foam, then add the chopped parsley and toss to combine. Season with plenty of salt and black pepper. Remove from the heat and keep warm.

For the red wine jus. Preheat the oven to 220°C/Gas Mark 7 (for the bacon). Put the wine and port in a saucepan with the shallots and bay leaves and boil to reduce to about one-tenth the original volume (about 50ml liquid).

Pass through a sieve into a clean pan and whisk in the butter, sugar, redcurrant jelly and seasoning to taste. Set aside, ready to reheat for serving.

For the liver. Cut the liver into four steak-sized portions about 2.5cm thick. Season them. Heat the oil in a frying pan and sear the liver for 4 minutes until nicely caramelised. Flip the liver over and add the butter to the pan. Cook for a further 4 minutes, basting the liver with the foaming butter. Remove the liver from the pan and leave to rest in a warm place for a few minutes (it will be medium and still slightly pink; if overcooked it will be tough).

For the bacon. While the liver is being cooked, spread the bacon rashers on a baking sheet and cook in the oven for about 8 minutes or until golden and crisp. Drain on kitchen paper.

To serve. Swipe the pea purée around the edge of four round shallow bowls or plates. Spoon the mushrooms at the end of the canal of pea created and set a kidney pudding alongside the mushrooms. Cut each liver steak in half on the diagonal; lay or stand tall on the plate and lay or stand the bacon on the diagonal on top of the liver. Spoon the sauce over and around the dish and garnish with pea shoots.

Rich and satisfying.

QUICK CASSOULET

SERVES 4

When I was a teenager I spent many summers in Sarlat, a small French market town, with my parents. One particularly memorable holiday there, I recall my dad buying a large round jar that held a family-sized portion of cassoulet. This jar came back with us to Cardiff as a sort of souvenir, where it lived in the fridge for about 5 years! Classic cassoulet, which has been around in one form or another for centuries, is a slow-cooked stew typically containing meat and beans – usually a type of sausage and confit duck leg, alongside haricot beans. Cassoulet in all its full-blown glory is a wonderful thing – this is a quicker version, perfect for a midweek meal or last-minute entertaining. Use premium quality sausages as this makes a real difference.

olive oil, for frying
4 thick Cumberland sausages
4 rashers streaky bacon, sliced
6 banana shallots, halved lengthways
1 courgette, sliced into discs
2 garlic cloves, lightly crushed with the
    back of a knife
250g cooking chorizo, diced
1 teaspoon chilli flakes
a few dashes of Tabasco sauce
1 x 400g can chopped tomatoes
1 x 400g can cannellini beans, drained
1 x 400g can butter beans, drained
1/2 x 460g jar roasted peppers, drained
    and sliced
250ml chicken stock
a small bunch of thyme, tied with string
salt and white pepper to taste

To finish
4 tablespoons chopped parsley
4 tablespoons finely grated Parmesan
1 tablespoon finely grated lemon zest
4 tablespoons dried breadcrumbs
Parmesan shavings, to garnish (optional)

In a wide flameproof casserole with a lid, heat a glug of olive oil, then gently brown the Cumberland sausages on all sides. Remove them and cut across in half; set aside.

Add the bacon to the pan and brown it, then add the halved shallots. When the shallots are slightly golden, remove them with a slotted spoon and set aside. Add the courgette and garlic to the bacon, with more olive oil if needed, and season with white pepper and a little salt. Cook for 3 minutes, then add the chorizo and stir well to combine. Stir in the chilli flakes and Tabasco. Fry for 4–5 minutes or until the chorizo is lightly browned. Add the canned tomatoes and beans, the roasted peppers and stock and stir to mix.

Return the sausages and shallots to the pan along with the bunch of thyme. Bring to the boil. Taste and adjust the seasoning, then cover and simmer gently for 30 minutes. Turn up the heat and cook with the lid slightly ajar for a further 10 minutes to reduce the sauce slightly.

Preheat the grill to medium. Combine the parsley, Parmesan, lemon zest and breadcrumbs. Check the cassoulet for seasoning, and remove and discard the bunch of thyme. Scatter the breadcrumb mixture evenly over the surface of the cassoulet to cover completely. Place under the grill for 8–10 minutes or until golden brown. Leave to rest for 5 minutes before serving in large bowls, garnished with Parmesan shavings if you like.

FENNEL MEATBALL PASTA WITH PEPERONATA SAUCE SERVES 4

Possibly my favourite recipe in this collection, I first made this dish while on holiday with my partner on the Isle of Anglesey. We spent a week over Valentine's Day cooped up in a self-catering lodge where I worked on recipe ideas and tried out the new dishes, with her as my official taster. This dish sums up the kind of food that I enjoy eating and the direction that I want my food to take. It's minimal in ingredients and complexity yet excels in delivering visual appeal and, most importantly, flavour.

400g dried pasta shapes such as
   lumaconi, penne or rigatoni
extra virgin olive oil, for drizzling
fennel fronds, to garnish (if available)

For the meatballs
olive oil, for frying
2 tablespoons fennel seeds
500g good-quality minced pork

For the sauce
2 red peppers
2 yellow peppers
about 100ml olive oil
1 red chilli
1 fat garlic clove (unpeeled)
1 tablespoon capers
5 fresh deli anchovies, drained
salt and white pepper to taste

For the meatballs. Heat a small saucepan and add 1 tablespoon olive oil with the fennel seeds. Cook gently for 2–3 minutes or until aromatic. Remove and drain off the excess oil, then add the seeds to the mince with some salt and pepper. Mix well. Shape into 12 equal-sized meatballs. Set aside in the fridge to firm up.

For the sauce. Preheat the oven to 220°C/Gas Mark 7. Place the whole peppers in a roasting tray and drizzle a little of the olive oil over them. Sprinkle with salt. Roast for 20 minutes. Toss the whole chilli and garlic clove in oil, then add to the roasting tray and roast for a further 15 minutes or until the skin on the peppers is blackened and blistered. Remove from the oven. Put the peppers in a bowl, cover tightly with clingfilm and set aside for 10 minutes. In the meantime, finely dice the roasted chilli, and slip the soft garlic flesh out of the skin. Set aside.

Peel the skins from the peppers, then slice them, discarding the stalks and seeds. Tip them into a blender along with the chilli, garlic, capers and anchovies. Blend the mixture to a smooth purée. Add 50ml of the olive oil and blend again. Check the consistency: if the sauce is too thick, add more olive oil. Season well with salt and pepper.

To finish the meatballs and pasta. Heat a large frying pan and add some olive oil. When the oil is hot, add the meatballs and brown them well all over. Turn down the heat and cook gently for 10 minutes. Meanwhile, cook the pasta in a large pan of boiling salted water according to the packet directions, until al dente; drain well.

To serve. Add the pepper sauce to the meatballs, then add the cooked pasta and fold together until coated with the sauce. Finish with a drizzle of extra virgin olive oil and a garnish of fennel fronds, if using.

Simple, yet so full in flavour.

PAN-ROASTED GINGER PORK LOIN,
ROAST POTATO, MULLED CIDER SAUCE, SALT-BAKED CARROTS, SPICED CABBAGE, GINGER CRUMB   SERVES 4

1 x 2.5kg boneless loin of pork, skin removed and reserved
4 tablespoons ground ginger
olive oil
a knob of butter
micro rocket, to garnish

For the onion sauce
2 large Spanish onions
200ml beef stock

For the mulled cider sauce
250ml dry cider
4 cloves
1 cinnamon stick
1 sprig of thyme
1 strip of orange peel
2 large cooking apples
a knob of butter
finely grated zest of 1/2 orange
2 teaspoons caster sugar
100g soft light brown sugar

For the ginger crumb
2 gingernut biscuits
3/4 teaspoon salt
3/4 teaspoon ground ginger

For the salt-baked carrots
500g salt
1 1/2 teaspoons caraway seeds, crushed
1 1/2 teaspoons coriander seeds, crushed
1 1/2 teaspoons fennel seeds, crushed
2 garlic cloves, chopped
2 egg whites

4 large carrots (preferably purple or heritage carrots)
olive oil, for frying
a large knob of butter

For the roast potatoes
4 large Maris Piper potatoes (all the same size)
300g goose fat
a few sprigs of thyme
1 garlic clove, lightly crushed

For the spiced cabbage
1 red onion, sliced
75g unsalted butter
1 small red cabbage, thinly sliced
150ml port
1 tablespoon redcurrant jelly
100g soft light brown sugar
50ml red wine vinegar
50ml balsamic vinegar
juice of 1 lemon
1 bay leaf
1 teaspoon grated fresh ginger
1 cinnamon stick

For the orange-glazed carrots
8 baby carrots
1 1/2 teaspoons olive oil
25g unsalted butter
100ml chicken stock
juice of 1 orange
salt and pepper to taste

For the onion sauce. Preheat the oven to 200°C/Gas Mark 6. Cut the unpeeled onions in half and place cut side down on a baking tray lined with greaseproof paper. Bake for 1 hour 10 minutes, or until very tender. Remove from the oven and squeeze each half to remove the flesh from the skin. Put the flesh into a saucepan, cover with water and bring to the boil. Boil to reduce to about one-tenth of the original volume. Pass through a chinois into a clean pan and reduce to a sticky syrup. Add the stock and boil to reduce by half. Season to taste and set aside, ready to reheat for serving.

For the mulled cider sauce. Bring the cider to the boil in a saucepan. Reduce to a simmer and add the spices, thyme and orange peel, then simmer gently for 5 minutes. Remove from the heat and set aside to infuse for 1 hour.

Meanwhile, peel and dice the apples, then soften in the butter in a hot pan. Add the orange zest and caster sugar and continue cooking to a pulpy texture. Stir in the brown sugar. Transfer to a food processor and blitz until smooth.

Strain the cider into a clean pan. Add the apple sauce and mix well. Set aside, ready to reheat for serving.

continued on page 212

continued from page 211

For the ginger crumb. Crush the ingredients to a fine crumb using a pestle and mortar. Set aside.

For the pork loin. Lay out a sheet of clingfilm large enough to wrap up the pork loin. Sprinkle the ground ginger evenly over the clingfilm. Roll the pork in the ginger to coat all over, then wrap tightly in the clingfilm. Place on a tray and set aside in the fridge for 1 hour. After an hour, unwrap the pork and cut across into four even pieces. Keep in a cool place until needed.

For the salt-baked carrots. Mix together the salt, crushed spices, garlic and egg whites in a large mixing bowl. Beat with your hand in a circular motion for about 5 minutes or until the mixture is well combined and malleable. Line a baking tray with greaseproof paper. For each carrot, place a handful of the salt mix on the tray, top with a carrot and cover with more salt mix, to enclose the carrot completely. Bake for 40 minutes.

Remove from the oven (turn it up to 220°C/Gas Mark 7 for the roast potatoes). Crack the salt crusts and remove the carrots. Peel them and slice each lengthways into eighths. Set aside until needed.

For the roast potatoes. Cut each potato into a thick rectangular shape (removing all the skin). Par-boil in a saucepan of boiling salted water for 8–10 minutes. Drain and scrape the sides gently with a fork. Heat the goose fat in a roasting tin in the oven until melted and slightly smoking. Add the potatoes with the thyme and garlic and roast for 30–40 minutes or until golden and crisp – turn them halfway through the roasting so they colour evenly. (While the potatoes are roasting, cook the cabbage, orange-glazed carrots and pork.)

For the spiced cabbage. Soften the onion in 25g of the butter in a large saucepan. Add the cabbage along with the other ingredients and remaining butter. Cook gently, stirring frequently, for about 40 minutes or until the cabbage is very tender and sticky. When ready, keep warm.

For the crackling. Preheat a second oven to 240°C/Gas Mark 9. Score the pork skin, then place on a baking tray. Season with salt and pepper and add a light drizzle of olive oil. Roast for 40 minutes or until browned and crisp. Cut into portions for serving.

For the orange-glazed carrots. Gently fry the baby carrots in the olive oil and butter in a pan until golden. Add the stock and simmer until it has evaporated and the carrots are tender and glazed. Add the orange juice and season to taste.

To finish the pork. Season the pieces of pork loin. Heat 1 tablespoon olive oil in an ovenproof frying pan and pan-roast the pork over a high heat for about 8 minutes on the rounded side until golden. (If your pan is too small you can slice the loin into two even log shapes.) Add the knob of butter and pan-roast for a further minute, spooning the foaming butter over the pork, then transfer the pan to the 220°C/Gas Mark 7 oven to finish cooking for 6 minutes. Remove from the oven and leave to rest for 10 minutes before serving.

To finish the salt-baked carrots. Heat a little olive oil in a hot frying pan and pan-roast the carrots for 3–4 minutes, turning them to colour evenly. Add the butter and continue cooking for 1 minute or so until golden. Keep hot.

To serve. Place a tablespoon of mulled cider sauce to the left on each plate. Set a roast potato alongside with a spoonful of cabbage and a salt-baked carrot. Add a mound of ginger crumb and the crackling. Set the pork on the cider sauce. Add the orange-glazed carrots and a spoonful of onion sauce. Garnish with micro rocket.

MasterChef highlights and lowlights?

I have so many highlights of my time during MasterChef: being at Mamma Agata's, cooking for previous winners, nailing the showstopper round, even meeting Larkin! But, my all time MasterChef highlight has to be making the final three. It was the target I'd set myself before entering the competition and doing so was a very proud moment for me.

Many will assume my lowlight was being so heavily criticised by Michelin-starred chef Marcus Wareing, but it wasn't. I used that experience to improve; it made me a better chef. My lowlight was not winning! I put so much into the competition and, more than anything, I wanted to win it for my mum. She was there for me at every round and she instilled in me a love of food from such a young age. Phoning Mum to tell her I hadn't won was one of the hardest things I've ever done.

Deep-frying has a reputation for being unhealthy, but there's no denying the flavour in a beautifully deep-fried fillet of fish, a meltingly sweet onion ring or, in this case, a crisp-fried ball of gooey risotto. It's an indulgent dish but the ultimate crowd-pleaser if you get it right. Arancini can be tricky – you have to make a risotto to the correct consistency so that it can form a ball without breaking its shape. If the risotto is too thin the arancini will break apart; too thick and the balls will be stodgy. Perfect arancini have a crisp outer coating with a light almost aerated risotto filling. I've used a classic combination of pea and ham here. You can make a vegetarian version by replacing the ham hock with asparagus.

For the arancini
65g butter
150g peas (preferably shelled fresh)
4 tablespoons freshly grated Parmesan
1 litre hot chicken stock
1 teaspoon grated nutmeg
1 tablespoon olive oil
1/2 white onion, finely diced
200g risotto rice
80ml white wine
75g boneless cooked ham hock
150g goat's cheese
plain flour, for dusting
2 eggs, beaten
300g fine fresh breadcrumbs
vegetable oil, for deep-frying

For the minted pea purée
1/2 onion, finely diced
1 garlic clove, finely sliced
25g unsalted butter
200g peas (preferably shelled fresh)
200ml vegetable stock
30 mint leaves
salt and black pepper

To garnish
4 unbroken egg yolks
boneless cooked ham hock, shredded
pea shoots
extra virgin olive oil

For the arancini. Begin by making the risotto for the arancini. Heat a large saucepan and add 25g of the butter followed by the peas. Gently soften the peas for 3–4 minutes, then remove from the heat. Spoon half the peas into a food processor and the rest into a bowl. Add 2 tablespoons of the Parmesan and a ladleful of the hot chicken stock to the processor, and season with the nutmeg and some salt and pepper. Blitz to a fine purée. Set aside, with the whole peas, until needed.

Return the saucepan to the heat and add another 25g butter along with the olive oil. When hot add the onion and soften for 4–5 minutes. Add the rice and then the wine and cook, stirring, until the wine has been absorbed. Stirring constantly, add the remaining stock, a ladleful at a time, allowing each addition of stock to be almost totally absorbed by the rice before adding the next – this process will take 20–30 minutes. When all the stock has been added, turn down the heat and stir in the pea purée along with the ham hock, the reserved whole peas, the rest of the Parmesan and the remaining 15g butter. Season with salt and pepper. The risotto should be a vibrant green. Remove from the heat, cover the pan and leave to cool completely. Once cooled, transfer to a non-reactive container with a lid and keep in the fridge overnight.

To make each arancini, take a small handful of the cold risotto and roll into a ball slightly larger than a golf ball. Press a dent through to the centre of the arancini using your finger and push in a rolled ball of goat's cheese, then mould the rice around this to seal the hole. Dust the ball in flour, then dip in beaten egg and, finally, coat in breadcrumbs. Repeat this with the remaining risotto, to make four arancini in all. Keep in the fridge until needed.

For the minted pea purée. Soften the onion and garlic in the butter in a small saucepan. Add the peas and stir well, then add the stock along with the mint leaves. Bring to the boil, then cover, remove from the heat and set aside for about 1 hour to allow the mint to flavour the peas. Tip the mixture into a food processor and blitz until smooth, then pass through a sieve into a clean pan. Season to taste. If the purée is too thin, simmer to reduce and thicken it slightly. Set aside, ready to reheat for serving.

To finish the arancini and egg yolks. Heat oil for deep-frying to 180°C. Also, bring a small saucepan of water to a rolling boil. Drop the arancini into the hot oil and deep-fry for 5–6 minutes until golden. Remove and drain on kitchen paper. Keep hot while you poach the egg yolks: gently immerse in the boiling water for 3 seconds, then carefully remove with a metal spoon and drain on kitchen paper.

To serve. Place a few tablespoons of pea purée at one end of each plate and use the back of the spoon to drag the purée into a trail. Place the arancini at one end and the poached egg yolk at the other. To garnish, mix the ham hock with the pea shoots, dress with extra virgin olive oil and seasoning, and add to the plates.

VENISON, SPRING GREENS, FONDANT POTATO
AND BÉARNAISE SAUCE   SERVES 4

For the Béarnaise sauce
3 shallots, finely chopped
5 black peppercorns
20g fresh tarragon, finely chopped
6 tablespoons white wine vinegar
3 large egg yolks
200g unsalted butter, melted

For the fondant potatoes
4 large Maris Piper potatoes
olive oil
a knob of unsalted butter
2 garlic cloves, crushed
1 large sprig of thyme
300–350ml chicken stock

For the tomatoes
150g cherry or plum tomatoes
   (ideally mixed colours)
100g unsmoked bacon lardons
olive oil

For the venison steaks
4 venison fillet steaks, 150g each
olive oil
a large knob of unsalted butter

For the spring greens
500g spring greens, finely sliced
olive oil
salt and black and white pepper to taste

For the Béarnaise sauce. Combine the shallots, peppercorns, half of the tarragon and the vinegar in a small pan with 1 tablespoon water. Bring to the boil and reduce for a couple of minutes until there is about 1 tablespoon of liquid remaining.

Put the egg yolks in a heatproof bowl, strain in the reduced vinegar mix and set over a pan of slowly simmering water. Whisk until frothy. Slowly add the melted butter while whisking constantly to make a thick sauce consistency. Add the remaining tarragon and season to taste. Remove from the heat. Leave the sauce in the bowl over the warm pan until ready to serve, stirring occasionally.

For the fondant potatoes. Peel the potatoes and cut out a round cylinder from each one using a 6cm diameter metal cutter. Neaten the top and bottom of each cylinder with a knife so they are flat. Heat a medium frying pan over a medium heat and add a splash of oil with the butter. Gently brown the potatoes for about 5 minutes on a flat side or until golden, then turn over and gently brown the other flat side for 5 minutes.

Add the garlic and thyme to the pan along with enough stock to come about halfway up the potatoes. Cover the pan and bring to a simmer, then cook for about 20 minutes, turning the potatoes over and basting with the stock every 5 minutes. Add more stock if the pan is running dry. When the potatoes are tender, remove from the heat and keep warm in the stock. (While the potatoes are cooking, you can prepare the other elements of the dish.)

For the tomatoes. Preheat the oven to 180°C/Gas Mark 4. Take a 5mm slice from the root end of each tomato and discard. Gently turn the tomatoes and bacon lardons in olive oil in a baking dish and season. Roast for 20–25 minutes.

For the venison steaks. Heat a heavy-based ovenproof frying pan. Season the venison steaks with salt and pepper, then rub olive oil all over them. Add a little oil to the pan, then add the steaks – they should sizzle immediately. Leave to sear for 2–3 minutes or until well browned, then turn the steaks over, add the butter to the pan and brown the other side. Continue cooking, basting the steaks continuously with the foaming butter and turning them, for 3–4 minutes. Transfer the pan to the oven, increasing the temperature to 220°C/Gas Mark 7, and cook for a final 2–3 minutes.

Remove the pan from the oven and transfer the steaks to a carving board. Leave to rest for at least 5 minutes while you prepare the spring greens.

For the spring greens. Steam the greens for 5 minutes or until tender. Remove from the steamer and dress with olive oil, salt and white pepper.

To serve. Gently lift the fondant potatoes from the pan and place one on each large plate. Add a mound of spring greens and scatter the lardons and cherry tomatoes around the edge of the plate. Cut each venison steak in half on the diagonal (it should be a beautiful medium-rare) and arrange beside the potato. Serve with the Béarnaise sauce.

I'm a sucker for tarragon. It's a glorious herb and can be used to give a warming sense of aniseed comfort to so many dishes – a hearty fish pie, charred ribeye steak or roast chicken, for example. In this dish, the flavour of the venison against the tarragon-rich Béarnaise is a joy. It's really important to get your pan really hot for the venison steak, so the outside is seared while a soft pink centre is retained. I created this dish for John and Gregg, to follow my citrus sea bass dish (see page 160), which it complements perfectly.

DALE WILLIAMS

ROAST BREAST OF GUINEA FOWL,
CONFIT LEG, BLACK PUDDING BONBON, PARSNIP, ASPARAGUS,
WHITE TRUFFLE CREAM SAUCE AND TRUFFLE SHAVINGS   SERVES 4

FROM THE SERIES, FINAL DISH

When I knew I was in the *MasterChef* Final, I couldn't wait to tell my mum and dad. Their support had been extraordinary and they were so proud of me. I wanted to be with them, to tell them in person and to see their expressions. But I was in London and they were back home in Cardiff. So I had to tell them over the phone. My family were all together waiting for the news. I wasn't sure what was going on for all the noise and commotion on the other end of the phone. But they were happy. My mum has always been my cooking inspiration – we're each other's sous chef – so when I came up with this dish I turned to my mum for some advice and her opinion on the components. It takes a lot of work and is quite complex to make, but it's a great dish that went on to be the main course in my Final menu.

2 guinea fowl
8 large asparagus spears
olive oil, for frying
150g unsalted butter
2 large parsnips (unpeeled)
leaves picked from a small bunch
    of tarragon
shavings of fresh Périgord truffle,
    to garnish (optional)

For the confit
700g duck fat
2 bay leaves
10 sprigs of soft thyme

For the bonbons
30g dried mixed mushrooms
2 rashers streaky bacon, roughly chopped
100g black pudding, roughly chopped
a small bunch of parsley, chopped
1 egg yolk
50g plain flour
3 eggs, beaten
100g panko breadcrumbs
vegetable oil, for deep-frying

For the asparagus mousse
12 large asparagus spears
50ml double cream
a splash of chicken stock
150g cream cheese

For the caramelised red onion
1 red onion, quartered
300g caster sugar
500ml red wine vinegar
olive oil, for frying

For the mushrooms
2 dried morels
olive oil, for frying
150g portabellini mushrooms, sliced
a knob of butter
1/2 banana shallot, diced
1 tablespoon chopped parsley
1 tablespoon chopped thyme
1 garlic clove, sliced
1 teaspoon Dijon mustard

For the white truffle sauce
50g button mushrooms, sliced
50g shallots, finely sliced
125g unsalted butter
125ml dry white wine
375ml white chicken stock
250ml double cream
25ml white truffle oil
salt and pepper to taste

For the guinea fowl. Remove the legs from the guinea fowl and separate the drumsticks and thighs. Reserve the crown (breasts on the bone) to roast.

For the confit. Scrape and tidy the drumstick bone, then place the drumsticks in a cold pan with the thighs. Add the duck fat, bay leaves and thyme and season with salt and pepper. Lay a sheet of baking parchment on top, then simmer on a low heat for 1 hour.

Remove the duck pieces from the fat and drain on kitchen paper (reserve the fat for the parsnips). Set the drumsticks aside, to be pan-fried later. Shred the meat from the thighs, discarding the skin, and mince coarsely in a blender or food processor (use this for the bonbons).

For the bonbons. Soak the dried mushrooms in a bowl of boiling water for 10 minutes to rehydrate; drain and chop finely. Mix together the mushrooms, bacon, black pudding, parsley and egg yolk in a bowl, using your hand, then add the minced confit thigh meat and combine well. Divide the mixture into four and roll each portion into a small ball, roughly the size of a golf ball. Dredge in flour, then dip in beaten egg and, finally, coat with breadcrumbs. Keep in the fridge until ready to deep-fry.

continued on page 220

continued from page 219

For the asparagus mousse. Cook the asparagus in a pan of boiling salted water until tender. Drain and transfer to a food processor. Add the cream and a little stock and blitz to a thick purée. Put the cream cheese in a bowl and beat to soften, then fold in the asparagus purée in two batches until thoroughly combined. Place in a squeezy bottle and set aside.

For the caramelised red onion. Drop the onion quarters into a pan of boiling water and boil for 10 minutes. Meanwhile, in a separate pan, dissolve the sugar in the vinegar and bring to the boil. Pour into a plastic container. Remove the onions from the pan of water with a slotted spoon and place in the container. Leave to marinate for 1 hour.

Before serving, drain the onion quarters, then caramelise in a hot frying pan with a little olive oil for 5 minutes on each side.

For the mushrooms. Soak the morels in a small bowl of boiling water for 10 minutes to rehydrate, then drain and finely dice. Heat a little oil in a frying pan and fry the sliced fresh mushrooms until golden. Add the butter, shallot and herbs and stir well, then add the garlic, mustard and seasoning to taste. Remove from the heat and stir in the diced morels. Set aside, ready to reheat for serving.

For the white truffle sauce. Sauté the mushrooms and shallots in 50g of the butter in a saucepan until softened and slightly browned. Add the white wine, bring to the boil and reduce by half. Add the chicken stock and reduce by two-thirds. Set aside.

Before serving, reheat the mixture, then add the cream and reduce to a sauce-like consistency. Pour into a blender or food processor and blend until smooth. Add the remaining butter and the truffle oil and blend until emulsified. Taste and adjust the seasoning, then keep warm.

For the asparagus. Trim the asparagus spears and thinly peel the stalks; set the peel aside. Slice the spears, then blanch in a pan of salted boiling water for 2 minutes. Drain. Just before serving, pan-fry with a little olive oil and butter until lightly browned.

For the confit parsnips. Preheat the oven to 200°C/Gas Mark 6. Par-boil the whole parsnips in a pan of boiling water until slightly softened. Drain and peel using a small knife, then cut each parsnip lengthways in half. Pour the duck fat reserved from the confit into an oven tray and heat in the oven. Add the parsnips and roast for 20–30 minutes or until golden brown. When ready, drain the parsnips on kitchen paper and keep warm.

For the roast guinea fowl. Heat an ovenproof frying pan, then pan-fry the crown, skin side down, in a little oil and butter for about 6 minutes or until the skin is golden and crisp. Turn skin side up and transfer to the oven with the parsnips. Roast for 20–25 minutes. When ready, remove from the oven and leave to rest for 15 minutes before cutting the breasts from the bone.

To finish the bonbons and confit legs. Heat oil for deep-frying to 180°C. Deep-fry the bonbons for 6 minutes or until golden all over. Drain on kitchen paper and keep hot. Deep-fry the picked tarragon leaves for 5 seconds; drain and reserve.

Heat enough olive oil in a frying pan for shallow frying, then add the confit drumsticks and fry for about 5 minutes to crisp the skin. Drain on kitchen paper.

To serve. Arrange a parsnip half and two asparagus spears on each plate at 45 degrees with 5cm between. Place a roast guinea fowl breast resting on the parsnip with a confit leg standing vertically alongside and a bonbon. Stand a caramelised onion quarter at the left of the breast and the mushrooms beside the bonbon. Add a spoonful of asparagus mousse to the plate. Layer the asparagus peels at the tip of the parsnip. Garnish with tarragon and finish with the truffle sauce and shavings of truffle, if using.

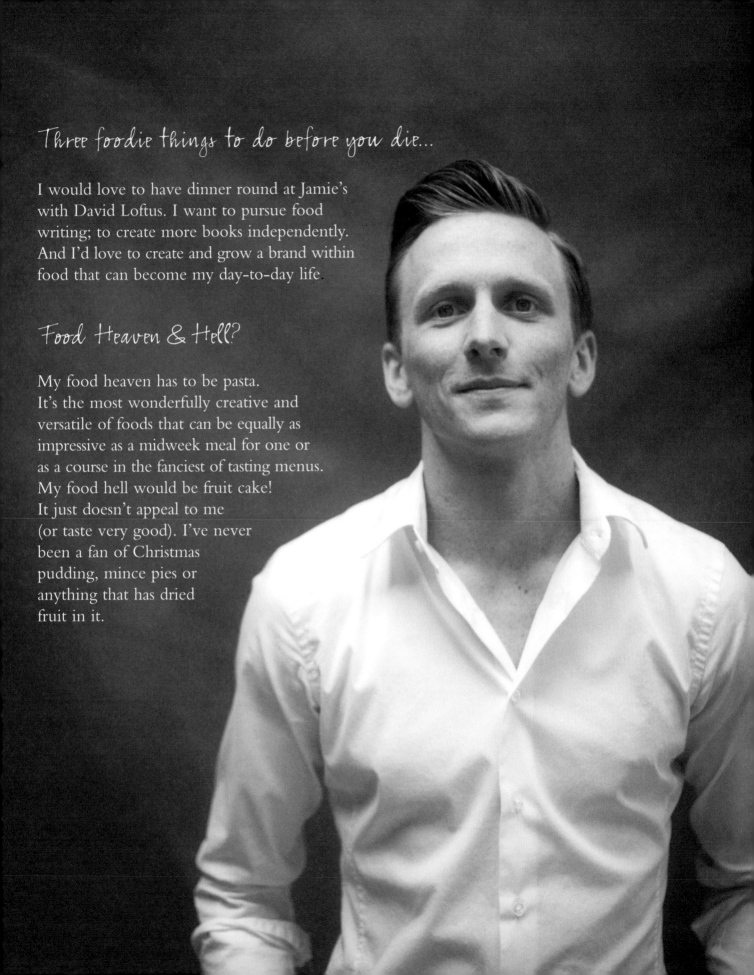

Three foodie things to do before you die...

I would love to have dinner round at Jamie's with David Loftus. I want to pursue food writing; to create more books independently. And I'd love to create and grow a brand within food that can become my day-to-day life.

Food Heaven & Hell?

My food heaven has to be pasta. It's the most wonderfully creative and versatile of foods that can be equally as impressive as a midweek meal for one or as a course in the fanciest of tasting menus. My food hell would be fruit cake! It just doesn't appeal to me (or taste very good). I've never been a fan of Christmas pudding, mince pies or anything that has dried fruit in it.

APPLE TARTE TATIN WITH CRÈME ANGLAISE

SERVES 4

For the tarte Tatin
4 heaped tablespoons golden caster sugar
5 Braeburn apples, peeled, quartered and cored
20g unsalted butter, cut into small pieces
500g all-butter puff pastry, thawed if frozen

For the crème anglaise
300ml full-fat milk
1 vanilla pod, split open
2 egg yolks
2 tablespoons caster sugar

For the tarte Tatin. Preheat the oven to 220°C/Gas Mark 7. Heat a 30cm tarte Tatin pan or a heavy-based ovenproof frying pan of about this size. Add the sugar to the pan and melt it, then cook until it caramelises. Add the apple quarters and turn them in the sugar to coat all over, then add the butter, dotting the pieces all over to be sure there is butter in every area. Leave to cook gently while you roll the pastry.

Roll out the pastry on a very lightly floured surface and cut to a round about 3cm larger all around than the top of the pan. If necessary, spread out the apples in one layer in the pan. Lay the pastry over the apples and tuck down inside the pan all around. Place in the oven and bake for 30 minutes or until the pastry is puffed and golden. Remove from the oven and allow to rest for 3 minutes before turning out on to a large lipped plate. Leave to cool.

For the crème anglaise. Pour the milk into a heavy-based saucepan. Scrape the seeds from the vanilla pod and add to the milk along with the empty pod. Heat the milk until it is almost boiling. Meanwhile, beat the egg yolks with the sugar in a bowl until pale and fluffy. Add the hot milk, whisking to combine. Pour into a clean pan and cook gently, stirring with a wooden spoon, until the custard is thick enough to coat the back of the spoon. Remove from the heat and pass through a sieve into a bowl. Cover the surface of the custard with clingfilm to prevent a skin from forming, then leave to cool.

To serve. Cut the tarte into wedges and serve with the crème anglaise.

BEIGNETS SOUFFLÉS WITH HAZELNUT CHOCOLATE SAUCE SERVES 6

I never used to have much of a sweet tooth. In fact, until recently, I rarely had a dessert when dining out. I would be much more likely to order the cheeseboard with a coffee. However, over the past couple of years I've found myself craving a sweet gooey dessert more and more, even at home. It always seems to be a craving for chocolate-based desserts – I prefer rich, dark chocolate with an almost bitter finish to milk chocolate. This dessert delivers on so many levels. Imagine a hot chocolate doughnut where you choose how much chocolate goes in the filling. The hazelnuts give the chocolate sauce another texture dimension, and I think you'll find the addition of cinnamon sugar over the hot soufflés a revelation.

For the beignets
75g unsalted butter
95g plain flour
3 large eggs, beaten
sunflower oil, for deep-frying
50g caster sugar
1 teaspoon ground cinnamon

For the chocolate sauce
200ml double cream
90g plain chocolate (minimum 70% cocoa solids)
25g hazelnuts, toasted and blitzed to a powder in a spice mill

For the beignets. Warm the butter with 225ml water in a saucepan over a low heat until the butter has melted. Turn up the heat and bring to the boil, then add the flour and beat vigorously until the mixture is smooth and leaves the sides of the pan. Remove from the heat and cool slightly before gradually beating in the eggs to make a smooth, glossy choux pastry.

Heat sunflower oil for deep-frying to 190°C. Working in batches so you don't overcrowd the pan, drop heaped teaspoonfuls of the choux pastry into the hot oil and deep-fry for about 5 minutes or until crisp and golden on all sides. Remove with a slotted spoon and drain on kitchen paper. You should make 24–30 beignets in all. Mix the caster sugar with the cinnamon in a shallow dish, add the beignets a few at a time and toss them gently until they are well coated.

For the chocolate sauce. Put the cream and chocolate into a small heatproof bowl. Set the bowl over a pan of lightly simmering water (ensure the base of the bowl does not touch the water) and gently stir until the chocolate has melted and the sauce is smooth and silky. Stir in the hazelnut powder.

To serve. Arrange the beignets on small plates with the sauce alongside for dipping. Sprinkle with a little extra cinnamon sugar.

This dessert delivers on so many levels.

CHOCOLATE TRUFFLE CAKE, HONEY AND MILK ICE CREAM, HAZELNUT BRITTLE, ORANGE ZEST SERVES 4

FROM THE SERIES

A stand-out moment for me in *MasterChef* was when the food critics offered such words of encouragement about this dessert, calling it 'accomplished', 'ten out of ten' and a 'triumph'. I had always thought of myself as a savoury man in the kitchen, avoiding making desserts if I could. However, after taking this dessert from concept through to delivery I became aware of how much I was growing with the competition. My truffle cake was the crowning moment, and I believe it's the dessert that won my place in the Final alongside Larkin and Nat. It was the perfect end to my menu for the critics on that day.

For the ice cream
300ml whole milk
6 egg yolks
115g caster sugar
3 tablespoons honey
300ml double cream

For the chocolate truffle cake
450g plain chocolate (minimum 70% cocoa solids), broken up
600ml double cream
cocoa powder, to garnish

For the hazelnut brittle
100g blanched (skinned) hazelnuts
200g caster sugar

For the orange zest and segments
4 oranges
200g caster sugar

For the ice cream. Heat the milk to scalding in a saucepan. Remove from the heat. Whisk the egg yolks with the sugar in a heatproof bowl until thick and creamy. Slowly whisk in the warm milk. Set the bowl over a pan of simmering water and stir with a wooden spoon until the custard will thinly coat the back of the spoon. Remove from the pan of water and stir in the honey. Leave to cool, then chill for 1 hour.

Whip the cream until soft peaks will form. Fold the cream into the cold honey custard. Pour into an ice cream machine and churn according to the manufacturer's instructions. Transfer to a freezer container and leave in the freezer until needed. If made ahead and very firm, remove from the freezer 15 minutes before serving and leave at room temperature to soften a bit.

For the truffle cake. Wrap doubled clingfilm around the sides and across the open base of four 5cm metal chef's/presentation rings. Set them on a tray. Melt the chocolate in a heatproof bowl set over a pan of simmering water. Meanwhile, warm the cream in a saucepan. Remove the bowl of chocolate from the hot water, then slowly stir in the warm cream. Transfer the mixture to a jug and pour into the moulds. Place in the fridge to set for 1 hour.

For the hazelnut brittle. Toast half of the hazelnuts in a frying pan. Remove from the heat and tip the nuts out of the pan. Set aside eight whole toasted hazelnuts for garnish. Put the rest of the toasted hazelnuts and the remaining (untoasted) hazelnuts in a mini food processor and pulse to a coarse crumb.

Melt the sugar in the frying pan, without stirring, then cook to a golden caramel colour. Add the hazelnut crumbs to the caramel and combine. Quickly pour on to a silicone mat in an even layer and set aside to cool and set.

For the orange zest and segments. Pare eight long, thin strips of coloured zest from the oranges; set aside. Cut the white pith from the oranges, then cut out the segments from the surrounding membrane; reserve the segments. Squeeze the juice from the membrane and cores into a saucepan.

Blanch the strips of zest in a small saucepan of boiling water two times, for 1 minute each time, refreshing in iced water after each blanching. Drain, then add the zest to the juice in the pan along with the sugar. Bring to the boil, stirring to dissolve the sugar, and simmer for about 10 minutes or until the zest is translucent. Remove from the heat. Using tongs transfer the strips of zest to a sheet of greaseproof paper and leave to cool and set. Add the orange segments to the remaining syrup and leave to macerate for at least 30 minutes.

To serve. For each serving, set a 6cm metal chef's/presentation ring on the plate and sift in cocoa powder to make a thin layer; lift off the ring. Remove the clingfilm from a truffle cake, then set it – in its mould – on top of or next to the cocoa powder disc, slightly overlapping it. Loosen the cake from its mould by briefly warming the outside of the ring with a cook's blowtorch, then gently lift off the ring. Dust the top of the cake with a little cocoa powder. Wrap each whole toasted hazelnut with a strip of orange zest and place on top of the cake. Break the brittle into shards and stick one or two into the top of the cake. Place two orange segments on the plate plus a quenelle of ice cream.

BAKED CUSTARD MERINGUES WITH GRAND MARNIER SAUCE SERVES 6

Think of a pavlova with a sweet creamy custard centre served with a warming, rich fruity sauce. That's what this adaptation of the classic crème brûlée is like. You use the egg whites to make an impressive meringue topping for the silky baked custards. They take a bit of practice but once mastered are the ultimate indulgent finish to a romantic meal for two. Be extravagant and complement the dessert with a glass of fine champagne.

For the baked custard
25g soft unsalted butter
125g caster sugar
500ml double cream
1 vanilla pod
6 egg yolks

For the meringue
3 egg whites
2 tablespoons caster sugar

For the Grand Marnier sauce
220g raspberries
70g icing sugar
50ml red wine
50ml Grand Marnier

For the custard. Preheat the oven to 150°C/Gas Mark 2. Use the soft butter to grease the inside of six deep ramekins (about 175ml capacity), then thinly coat them with sugar, using 25g of the caster sugar.

Pour the cream into a saucepan set over a medium heat. Split the vanilla pod lengthways and scrape the seeds into the cream; add the empty pod too. Heat the cream to boiling point, then reduce the heat and simmer gently for about 5 minutes.

Beat the remaining 100g caster sugar with the egg yolks in a heatproof bowl until pale and fluffy. Bring the cream back to boiling point. Remove the vanilla pod, then pour the cream over the yolk mixture, whisking constantly. Strain the mixture through a fine sieve into a large jug. Pour into the ramekins (they should be about two-thirds full).

Set the ramekins in a large roasting tray and pour enough hot water into the tray to come halfway up the sides of the ramekins. Place in the oven and bake for about 40 minutes or until the custards are just starting to set but are still a bit wobbly in the middle. Remove the custards from the oven. Pour off the water from the roasting tray, then return the custards to the tray. Leave the oven on.

For the meringue. In a spotlessly clean bowl, whisk the egg whites to soft peak stage. Gradually whisk in the sugar. Spoon the mixture into a piping bag fitted with a star tube. Working quickly, pipe the meringue on to the custards to form peaks. Return the custards to the oven to bake for 8–10 minutes or until the meringue is lightly golden. Leave to cool, to serve at room temperature.

For the sauce. Blitz the raspberries in a food processor to make a purée, then pass this through a sieve into a clean pan. Add the icing sugar, wine and Grand Marnier and stir to mix. Bring to a simmer and cook for 5 minutes or until slightly reduced. Remove from the heat and set aside, ready to reheat when needed.

To serve. Serve the custards with the hot raspberry sauce.

The ultimate indulgent finish to a meal.

COCONUT PANNACOTTA WITH CHAMPAGNE FRUITS SERVES 4

It's fair to say I like a cheeky drink with my food, a splash of brandy on my crêpes, a glug of white in my risotto or a bottle of lager in my batter. Desserts are no exception. In fact, they're possibly the one area of the kitchen where you can be most experimental with a tipple. This dessert is certainly extravagant and you might want to save it for a special occasion, but rest assured if you go all out to buy a good-quality champagne it will make all the difference to the finished dish. Champagne is the drink for celebrating, whether to introduce a toast or to see in the New Year. The *MasterChef* competition has been one of the most turbulent and exhausting yet rewarding and fun experiences of my life. This dish was inspired by my desire to go out with a bang and to celebrate what would – *at the very least* – be a wonderful and memorable chapter of my life.

For the pannacotta
2 bronze gelatine leaves
50ml milk
150ml double cream
25g caster sugar
1 vanilla pod, split open
85g white chocolate, broken up
200ml coconut milk

For the syrup
300ml champagne
200g caster sugar
a 1cm piece fresh ginger, peeled and
    finely sliced
a pinch of ground cinnamon
1/2 vanilla pod, split open

For the fruits
125g ripe strawberries, cut into quarters
1 large ripe mango, sliced
2 ripe kiwi fruits, thickly sliced
flesh from 1 small pineapple, cut into chunks

For the coconut macaroons
1 large egg white
70g caster sugar
70g desiccated coconut

To garnish
20g desiccated coconut, toasted
sprigs of micro basil

For the pannacotta. Soak the gelatine in a small bowl of cold water for 5 minutes or until softened. Meanwhile, heat the milk, cream, sugar and vanilla pod in a heavy-based saucepan to simmering point. Remove from the heat. Put the white chocolate and coconut milk in a heatproof bowl and set over a pan of simmering water to melt. Remove the bowl from the heat. Strain the milk and cream mixture over the chocolate mix. Squeeze the gelatine leaves to remove excess water, then add to the mixture and whisk until melted. Divide among four 100ml ramekins. Place in the fridge to set for at least 2 hours.

For the syrup. Combine all the ingredients in a saucepan and bring to the boil, then reduce for 5 minutes. Strain through a fine sieve into a jug.

For the fruits. Pour a quarter of the syrup into a clean saucepan and heat gently. Add the strawberries and cook for 1 minute, then transfer the strawberries and syrup to a container with a lid. Repeat this process with the mango and kiwi. Add the pineapple to the last of the syrup and cook for 10 minutes, then place in a container. Leave the fruits to macerate in their syrups until needed.

For the coconut macaroons. Preheat the oven to 150°C/Gas Mark 2. Line a flat baking tray with baking parchment. Whisk the egg white in a clean bowl until soft peaks will form. Gradually whisk in the sugar, whisking to stiff peaks. Fold in the coconut in two batches. Spoon the macaroon mixture into a piping bag fitted with a plain nozzle and pipe small mounds about 2.5cm in size on to the baking tray. Bake for 10 minutes. Allow to cool on the baking tray.

To serve. Drain the fruits, reserving the syrup. Using a cook's blowtorch, briefly warm the sides of each ramekin, then gently ease out the pannacotta on to a serving plate. Arrange the fruits around the pannacotta and set the macaroons in and around the fruits. Drizzle the syrup over the fruits and finish the pannacotta with a sprinkling of toasted coconut. Garnish with sprigs of basil.

DAD'S ROSE WATER RICE PUDDING, HONEY-BAKED FIGS, PISTACHIOS SERVES 4

A family favourite for many years, this rice pudding seems to play with your senses and tastebuds. The addition of rose water against a backdrop of coconut milk and pistachios transforms the classic rice pudding to a fine dining level. Adding baked fresh figs brings another dimension. It's a brilliant dessert. You can make it in advance to serve when needed.

For the rice pudding
200ml double cream
200ml coconut milk
200g pudding rice
seeds from 8 cardamom pods
700ml whole milk
100g caster sugar
3 tablespoons rose water

For the figs
8 large fresh figs
2 tablespoons honey
100ml good-quality port

To garnish
30g shelled pistachios, toasted and crushed

For the rice pudding. Preheat the oven to 200°C/Gas Mark 6. Heat a heavy-based non-stick saucepan over a low heat. Combine the cream and coconut milk in a measuring jug, then pour two-thirds of the mixture into the pan. Add the rice and cardamom seeds and stir well. Cook for a few minutes before adding the milk and sugar, then cook on a low heat, stirring occasionally, for 40–45 minutes or until the rice grains are soft and the liquid has been absorbed. Add the remaining cream and coconut mixture along with the rose water and stir to mix.

For the figs. While the rice pudding is cooking, cut a deep cross vertically in each fig, nearly to the bottom, then gently squeeze the sides to expose the flesh. Place the figs in a baking dish with a lid and drizzle over the honey and port. Cover the dish and bake for about 20 minutes.

To serve. Spoon the rice pudding into deep bowls and set two figs on top. Scatter the crushed pistachios over the figs. Serve the syrup from the baking dish in a small jug.

A firm family favourite.

Index

Southern-fried 107

soy-poached with soy reduction 103–4

the triple crown 107

chicory: pan-roasted pigeon with orange braised lentils, chicory and hazelnuts 53

chilli:

chilli beef and pineapple fried rice 115

Little J's chilli crab noodles 184

the Chinese three roast dinner 133–4

chips:

fries 195–6

thick-cut 143

chocolate:

beignets soufflés with hazelnut chocolate sauce 224

chocolate and hazelnut crumble tart with rippled Chantilly cream and raspberry coulis 67

chocolate mojito 155

chocolate pannacotta with caramelised pears and hazelnut biscuits 79

chocolate soufflé and vanilla cream 156

chocolate truffle cake, honey and milk ice cream, hazelnut brittle, orange zest 227

rosemary and chocolate fondant with an orange Chantilly cream 80

chorizo:

chorizo and anchovy pappardelle 191

guinea fowl and lobster smoked paella with citrus air 139–140

pan-roasted chicken and bubbling goat's cheese with balsamic tomatoes and a courgette salad 192

quick cassoulet 207

red mullet ballotine with chorizo, olive, tomato and tapenade 179

chrysanthemum greens: braised pork belly in rose wine with chrysanthemum, taro, lotus root crisps and a fennel kimchi 129

cider:

pan-roasted ginger pork loin, roast potato, mulled cider sauce, salt-baked carrots, spiced cabbage, ginger crumb 211–12

roast and braised suckling pig, with fondant potato, celeriac purée, cavolo nero in a cider orange jus 125–6

citrus fruits:

guinea fowl and lobster smoked paella with citrus air 139–140

sea bass, citrus fruits and samphire with braised fennel 160

clams:

Dover sole en papillote with julienne of fennel, New Zealand clams and a Thai basil pesto 164

guinea fowl and lobster smoked paella with citrus air 139–140

pan-fried cod with clams, chargrilled and puréed cauliflower 12

saffron clams marinière, mini baguette 187

cockles:

pan-fried halibut, cockles and peanuts 87

rabbit loin wrapped in Serrano ham with cockles, cauliflower purée, samphire and a cockle vinaigrette 62

stir-fried cockles 103–4

coconut:

chocolate mojito 155

coconut pannacotta with Champagne fruits 231

pan-fried halibut, cockles and peanuts 87

rice pudding with blueberry compote and macadamia nuts 68

rose water rice pudding, honey-baked figs, pistachios 232

cod:

loin with fragrant curry sauce and coriander rice 171

pan-fried with clams, chargrilled and puréed cauliflower 12

smoked with a mussel and vegetable broth, anchovy puffs and pesto 168

confit:

Asian 'smoky' confit salmon with caviar 96

pan-fried duck breast, confit duck spring roll, pak choi, sweet potato purée and a star anise caramel dressing 144

quail ballotine, quail leg confit, crisp quail's egg, wild mushrooms and a quail jus 57–8

roast breast of guinea fowl, confit leg, black pudding bonbon, parsnip, asparagus, white truffle cream sauce and truffle shavings 219–20

congee: ham hock congee with sardines and Chinese crullers 130

coriander and orange pan-fried scallops with beetroot purée, beetroot wedges and samphire 26

courgette flowers: crab-filled courgette flowers with lemon mayonnaise 32

courgettes:

fillet of salmon with butter bean and saffron stew, Ibérico ham and charred courgette 172

pan-roasted chicken and bubbling goat's cheese with balsamic tomatoes and a courgette salad 192

couscous: pan-fried sea bass with cauliflower purée, cauliflower couscous and tempura cauliflower 15

crab:

crab-filled courgette flowers with lemon mayonnaise 32

crab risotto, Parmesan snap 183

Little J's chilli crab noodles 184

pan-fried sea bass with fennel, mini crab bonbons and a sauce vierge 16

steamed egg with crab 103–4

cream: see also mascarpone

orange Chantilly 80

rippled Chantilly 67

vanilla cream 156

crème anglaise 223

cucumber:

candied 155

cured mackerel, smoked mackerel pâté, cucumber, pickled mushrooms, pomegranate vinaigrette 175–6

mackerel with smoked eel and cucumber mousse and black bean purée 99

curry:

cod loin with fragrant curry sauce and coriander rice 171

duck curry served with candied orange pilau rice and thick-cut chips 143

grilled aubergine with onion bhajis and Bombay aloo 100

custard:

apple tarte tatin, crème anglaise 223

baked custard meringues with Grand Marnier sauce 228

Dover sole:

en papillote with julienne of fennel, New Zealand clams and a Thai basil pesto 164

with ginger and spring onions 88

dressings: see also mayonnaise; vinaigrette

soy 96

star anise caramel 144

teriyaki 91

Thousand Island 107

duck:

the Chinese three roast dinner 133–4

curry served with candied orange pilau rice and thick-cut chips 143

pan-fried breast, confit duck spring roll, pak choi, sweet potato purée and a star anise caramel dressing 144

pan-roasted breast with mini fondant potatoes, carrot and cumin purée and a red port jus 50

dukkah 61

e

eel: mackerel with smoked eel and cucumber mousse and black bean purée 99

eggs:

poached yolks 215

quail ballotine, quail leg confit, crisp quail's egg, wild mushrooms and a quail jus 57–8

roast pork belly, sous-vide pork tenderloin, black pudding Scotch egg, pomme purée, caramelised baby shallots, baby carrots, apple sauce and honey mustard sauce 44–6

steamed egg with crab 103–4

fennel:

braised pork belly in rose wine with chrysanthemum, taro, lotus root crisps and a fennel kimchi 129

Dover sole en papillote with julienne of fennel, New Zealand clams and a Thai basil pesto 164

fennel meatball pasta with peperonata sauce 208

lobster tail, fennel purée, compressed fennel, orange gel, orange beurre blanc, lobster caviar and lobster oil 35–6

sea bass, citrus fruits and samphire with braised fennel 160

sea bass with fennel, mini crab bonbons and a sauce vierge 16

sea bream fillet with langoustine, braised fennel, caramelised fennel and a langoustine sauce 21

sea trout with pomegranate and fennel salad and a teriyaki dressing 91

squid with squid ink sauce, Serrano ham crisps, fennel pollen and fennel 25

figs:

fig and frangipane tart with an orange mascarpone cream 71

rose water rice pudding, honey-baked figs, pistachios 232

fillet steak:

in black bean sauce, pak choi, with asparagus fried rice 112

tartare and seared scallop with hoisin sauce and Asian pear 116

fish:

Asian 'smoky' confit salmon with caviar 96

chorizo and anchovy pappardelle 191

cod loin with fragrant curry sauce and coriander rice 171

cod with clams, chargrilled and puréed cauliflower 12

cured mackerel, smoked mackerel pâté, cucumber, pickled mushrooms, pomegranate vinaigrette 175–6

Dover sole en papillote with julienne of fennel, New Zealand clams and a Thai basil pesto 164

Dover sole, ginger and spring onions 88

fillet of salmon with butter bean and saffron stew, Ibérico ham and charred courgette 172

hake, spinach purée, kale, chargrilled broccoli and pesto 163

halibut, cockles and peanuts 87

ham hock congee with sardines and Chinese crullers 130

stir-fried cockles 103–4

shallots:

beef teppanyaki with confit shallot and shallot purée 111

roast pork belly, sous-vide pork tenderloin, black pudding Scotch egg, pomme purée, caramelised baby shallots, baby carrots, apple sauce and honey mustard sauce 44–6

sharon fruit: Greek honey frozen yoghurt with pistachio meringue, caramelised sharon fruit and blackberry sauce 72

shiitake mushrooms: pan-fried wild sea bass, pork belly and shiitake mushroom wontons 92

Singapore chicken and udon noodle hot wok 108

smoked cod with a mussel and vegetable broth, anchovy puffs and pesto 168

sole, Dover:

en papillote with julienne of fennel, New Zealand clams and a Thai basil pesto 164

with ginger and spring onions 88

soufflé:

chocolate soufflé and vanilla cream 156

raspberry soufflé with peach ice cream 76

soups:

butternut squash with roasted tomato focaccia 188

lemongrass consommé 92

pan-fried wild halibut fillet, wild mushroom consommé, wild mushrooms, truffle and spinach 22

smoked cod with a mussel and vegetable broth, anchovy puffs and pesto 168

spiced plum tarte tatin with thyme ice cream 83

spinach:

chicken Kiev with a summer salad 199

pan-fried hake, spinach purée, kale, chargrilled broccoli and pesto 163

pan-fried wild halibut fillet, wild mushroom consommé, wild mushrooms, truffle and spinach 22

spring onions: Dover sole, ginger and spring onions 88

squid with squid ink sauce, Serrano ham crisps, fennel pollen and fennel 25

steak:

chilli beef and pineapple fried rice 115

fillet steak in black bean sauce, pak choi, with asparagus fried rice 112

fillet steak tartare and seared scallop with hoisin sauce and Asian pear 116

stock:

crab 183

fish 21

strawberries: coconut pannacotta with Champagne fruits 231

suckling pig roast and braised, with

fondant potato, celeriac purée, cavolo nero in a cider orange jus 125–6

sweet potatoes: pan-fried duck breast, confit duck spring roll, pak choi, sweet potato purée and a star anise caramel dressing 144

tapenade: red mullet ballotine with chorizo, olive, tomato and tapenade 179

taro: braised pork belly in rose wine with chrysanthemum, taro, lotus root crisps and a fennel kimchi 129

tarts:

apple tarte tatin, crème anglaise 223

chocolate and hazelnut crumble tart with rippled Chantilly cream and raspberry coulis 67

fig and frangipane tart with an orange mascarpone cream 71

lemon tart 151

spiced plum tarte tatin with thyme ice cream 83

Thousand Island dressing 107

thyme: spiced plum tarte tatin with thyme ice cream 83

tofu sheet rolls 103–4

tomatoes:

chorizo and anchovy pappardelle 191

Dover sole en papillote with julienne of fennel, New Zealand clams and a Thai basil pesto 164

pan-roasted chicken and bubbling goat's cheese with balsamic tomatoes and a courgette salad 192

quick cassoulet 207

red mullet ballotine with chorizo, olive, tomato and tapenade 179

spicy ketchup 179

venison, spring greens, fondant potato and béarnaise sauce 216

the triple crown 107

trout: pan-fried sea trout with pomegranate and fennel salad and a teriyaki dressing 91

truffles:

pan-fried wild halibut fillet, wild mushroom consommé, wild mushrooms, truffle and spinach 22

roast breast of guinea fowl, confit leg, black pudding bonbon, parsnip, asparagus, white truffle cream sauce and truffle shavings 219–20

vanilla: chocolate soufflé and vanilla cream 156

vegetable spring rolls 103–4

venison:

with dukkah, butternut squash purée & spiced pomegranate pearl barley 61

sashimi with tobacco-infused Peking sauce and wasabi mayonnaise 136

with spring greens, fondant potato and béarnaise sauce 216

vinaigrette: *see also* dressings

classic 199

cockles 62

mirin 99

pomegranate 175–6

wasabi mayonnaise 136

wine: sangria (fruit with orange jelly and red wine jus) 152

wontons: pan-fried wild sea bass, pork belly and shiitake mushroom wontons 92

yoghurt: Greek honey frozen yoghurt with pistachio meringue, caramelised sharon fruit and blackberry sauce 72

MasterChef

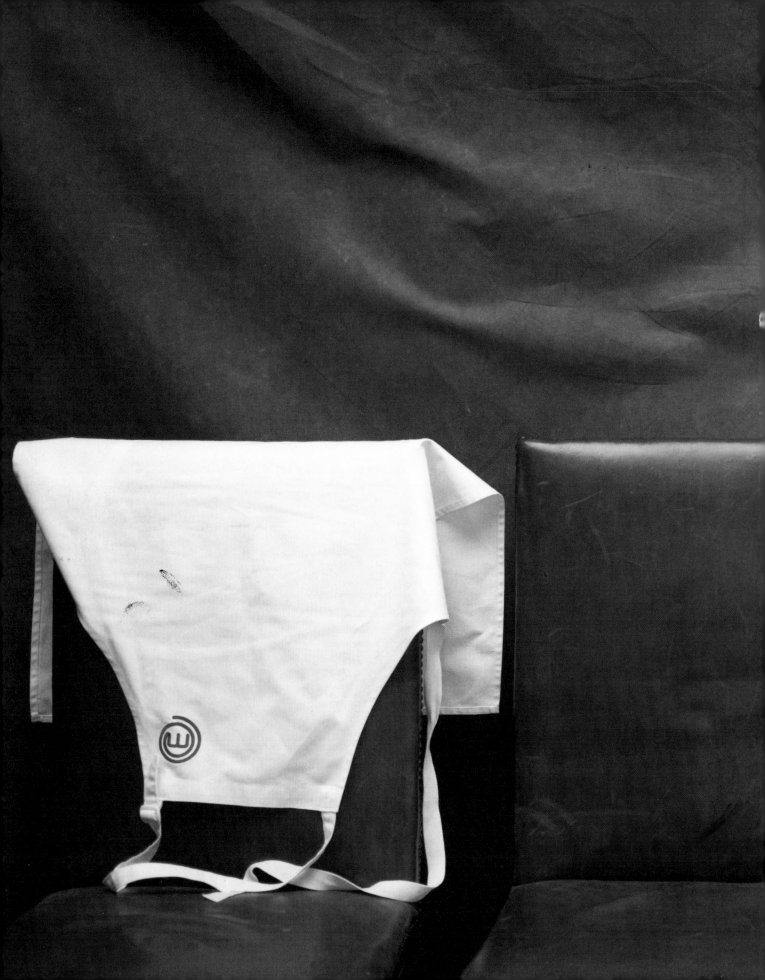